THE CLOUD OF UNKNOWING

Reflections of the Contemplative Path

Mary Beth Bradford

Copyright © 2023 Mary Beth Bradford

All rights reserved

No part of this book may be reproduced, or stored in a retrieval system, or transmitted in any form or by any means, electronic, mechanical, photocopying, recording, or otherwise, without express written permission of the author.

For Beth Ann, who encouraged me
For Sister Madeline, who showed me Catholicism I never knew
For Dad, who was the perfect model of God's unconditional love

PREFACE

This book will challenge you. At times, you'll be tempted to throw it across the room. I know I have. That's because it confronts much of the conditioning of modern culture about who God is.

I was a little—no, very much—turned off by the book at first. How could this be such a fantastic text about contemplation when it keeps telling me what a horrible wretch I was? I even disagreed with some of it, and perhaps there are parts I still do. I became a little—no, very much—frustrated by some of the rather abstract ideas. Why was the author so preoccupied with words like "up?"

I gave it a good read just to say I read it but then moved on to other texts about Centering Prayer and emotional attachment. I picked it up a little later, once I knew a little more about contemplation. Thankfully, Thomas Merton was able to elucidate contemplation much better than the anonymous author could. Using that lens allowed me to enjoy it a little more. I still found the text to be rather opaque, but I got a little more out of it. I read it a third time a few years later, taking my time with each chapter to try to absorb the deeper meaning.

My interest in *The Cloud* was when I saw an e-course for the text. Three days a week for a month I would get an email that would offer a snippet from part of *The Cloud* and the instructor illuminated that snippet. It was nice to get a little more background about the text, but it only covered a handful of the 75 chapters.

That course, however, sparked me to take a little deeper investigation of my own. Because I had been working at a university at the time—a Catholic one—I had access to several copies of The Cloud from the university library. I checked all of them out and spent almost three months with it, picking apart a chapter a day to piece together the essence. I then reflected on each chapter, particularly how a theme or sentence might speak to us today. Or I saw parallels with some Eastern traditions. I published my reflections twice a week on my Substack blog, "The Contemplative Path."

Then I wondered, "How can I make this accessible for people today?" In our distracted world that finds it difficult to pay attention, how can you take such a complex text and distill its meaning without losing it?

So I turned to something controversial today—artificial intelligence. Rather than taking the Gallacher version that includes Middle English (and making my eyes crossed), I turned to Evelyn Underhill, who put forth her version in 1922, before copyright laws existed. I would take a chapter and run it through my AI software to simplify the text. In some places, it would miss the point, so I would return to Underhill's for clarification. I would also resort to my original book from William Johnston and my favorite interpretation from Clifton Wolters.

I hope that this version of *The Cloud of Unknowing* will serve as an appetizer for the feast that is contemplation. If the first few chapters don't make sense, keep reading. The author even suggests this because some ideas come full circle towards the end. If the text upon first reading still sounds too esoteric for you, take it to prayer, then put it away for a few years. Then try it again. After a while, it will grow on you. It will transform you. Most of all, it will bring you into a closer relationship with God.

INTRODUCTION

I suck at praying out loud. At the end of many of my Bible studies, we would go around the table offering prayers. So many women would utter the most beautiful words. When it was my turn, I would just feel stupid. It wasn't that I feared public speaking, but rather I didn't know what to say.

I would utter word salad like, "Thank you God for giving us this time together to know you." Not original.

The many Catholic prayers ascribed to a particular saint or petition really move many people. Many people hold a strong devotion to Mary, and they will say a Hail Mary or a rosary and feel uplifted. I'm not one of them.

Even my personal prayers sounded like complaints and ruminations. God, why can't you get this guy to like me? Please give me this job. It was so much "pretty please" and "thank you" and didn't feel like a conversation with God. I just wanted to tell God that my idea of how things should be was much better than the way they were.

These days, our concept of "prayer" might sound a lot like this. Or we might believe "prayer" is something only religious people do. It wasn't until I came across contemplative traditions that I realized that prayer can be an experience. Yes, an experience.

With so many people leaving organized religion these days, people are yearning for a spiritual connection. Sure, they might find sugar substitutes of self-help that might give them temporary connection, but spiritual connection happens on a much deeper, profound level. Once you have a taste of it—what mystics call "awakening," you know there's something much richer than the world has to offer.

The Contemplative Tradition

The Cloud of Unknowing is one of those texts in the contemplative (or mystical) tradition, which can be found in Catholicism, Orthodox Christianity, and some Protestant denominations. It is often contrasted with more active forms of prayer, such as petitionary prayer or intercession, which involve making requests of God.

Christian contemplation has many forms of entry such as using scripture, sacred images, or other spiritual texts as a focus for meditation. It may also involve practices such as centering prayer, which involves repeating a word or phrase as a means of quieting the mind and opening oneself to God's presence. Or it might involve lectio divina, which is a Benedictine practice of entering into scripture rather than studying it.

The concept of contemplation is different from what you might understand. Typically, when we "contemplate" something, we mull over something, reflect, and consider other alternatives. Contemplation described in this tradition is about moving distracting thoughts away. This is similar to the second sutra in Patanjali's Yoga Sutras: Yogas citta vrtti nirodhah, which means stilling the excess chatter in your mind. Ira Progoff writes, "This means the control of thoughts arising from contact with other persons and objects; and the control of thoughts arising from within, fantasies and imaginings, desires and beliefs."[1] However, this pushing away of thoughts isn't contemplation but it prepares us for the entry.

The Cloud also reminds us not to look for sensory experiences. We don't aim to feel good during contemplative practices, although that might be a secondary outcome. I know that some traditions and practices will have people whipped into a frenzy. They're bodily experiences, such as a kundalini release of energy. That's not what we're talking about here. "[T]he author insists that true contemplation is found in the total forgetfulness of self and preoccupation with God; there is no search for experience, only a search for God."[2] In other words, looking for evidence of God through sensation is a mistake. Instead, we reach beyond the physical and direct ourselves inward.

Clifton Wolters gives a good description of contemplation. "Contemplation is not the pleasant reaction to a celestial sunset, nor is it the perpetual twitter of heavenly birdsong. It is not even an emotion. It is the awareness of God, known and loved at the core of one's being."[3] Wolters later says that most mystics cannot describe the bliss of contemplation. Instead, they offer words that point to the path. That's why via negativa and via positiva work together—we use words to point but recognize that words are insufficient.

Via Negativa in The Cloud

The author of the Cloud of Unknowing was heavily influenced by the writings of Pseudo-Dionysus. Pseudo-Dionysius, also known as the Areopagite, was a Christian theologian who wrote in the late 5th or early 6th century AD. The name "Pseudo-Dionysius" is a modern label given to the author, as his true identity is unknown, but he was attributed to the biblical figure of Dionysius the Areopagite who was converted by St. Paul. The author refers to him as "St. Denis" in Chapter 70.

Pseudo-Dionysius's theology emphasized the idea of God as beyond all human comprehension, and his works were intended to lead the reader toward a mystical experience of the divine. He believed that the path to union with God required a process of purification and enlightenment, culminating in a state of contemplation that transcends the limits of human knowledge.

Pseudo-Dionysis adopts the idea of *via negativa*, which is a perspective adopted by many contemplatives. *Via positiva* is much more common in religious and spiritual traditions in the West. *Via positiva* in theology refers to the positive way of speaking about God, which emphasizes God's attributes and qualities. This approach seeks to describe God's positive attributes, such as God's love, mercy, justice, and omnipotence. It attempts to provide a positive understanding of God by affirming what God is and what God can do.

On the other hand, *via negativa* in theology refers to the negative way of speaking about God, which emphasizes what God is not, or what God does not possess. This approach seeks to describe God's nature by negating human limitations and imperfections. It emphasizes the limitations of human language and concepts in describing God and asserts that God transcends human understanding.

The *via negativa* approach in theology stresses that human language and concepts are inadequate to fully grasp the nature of God and that our attempts to describe God through positive attributes or qualities can limit our understanding of God. The *via negativa* approach seeks to move beyond human language and concepts to a more profound and transcendent understanding of God.

It's not that we adopt one perspective and eschew the other. We use words and images, as the author does, to describe contemplation, but those words and images only point to the experience but aren't the experience itself. I've heard a metaphor for the moon that is helpful. For someone who is blind, we can use words to describe the beauty of the moon, but those words are inadequate to describe the experience of seeing it. Contemplatives will say that we must remove our spiritual blindness so we can experience God beyond the senses.

The anonymous author

The author of *The Cloud of Unknowing* remains anonymous to this day. Based on his use of language, scholars believe he was either a monk or a rural pastor living around Nottingham, England. The text was written in the late 14th century during intense political upheaval. The Black Death pandemic had already wiped out about a third of the population in England.

Although the author wrote other books, *The Cloud of Unknowing* is the most noted. The fact that the author chose to remain anonymous emphasizes one of the key themes in *The Cloud*—humility. The author's name might have been etched in history along with the likes of St. Augustine, St. Teresa of Avila, St. John of the Cross, or St. Thomas Aquinas, but instead, he chose to emphasize the work of contemplation over any credentials he might have obtained. In this regard, the author provides a stark contrast from what we see today—the need to be seen and heard or the need to get credit for our work.

How to use this book

One very important point here about *The Cloud of Unknowing*—it's not an instruction book on contemplation. If that's what you're looking for, you'll be very disappointed. Granted, the author gives suggestions about mantras and how to deal with nagging thoughts, but *The Cloud* is more of a book of encouragement to stay on the contemplative path, or what he calls "work." Contemplation arrives when God wants it to. It's a state of being rather than a destination. Centering Prayer, *lectio divina*, or even yoga practices might serve as runways but don't guarantee you'll take flight.

You'll notice the translation of each chapter is written first then followed by my reflection. At times, I'll clarify some of the sections that might seem opaque. Sometimes I'll pull from my study of yoga, Buddhism, or Taoism. Other times, I relate to something that's happening in modern times. And yet others will be elaborating on a specific theme that might provide some inspiration for you.

You could read the entire book in one sitting, but that might be too much all at once. You might not get the opportunity to let certain themes sink in deeply. Instead, use this book as a way of taking a break from worldly ways of doing things. Rather than try to get to the end, read until something stirs you, then sit with it for a while. I suggest taking a chapter a day to sip and savor. You might also like to reflect on that chapter in writing the way I did. Then go out and notice. Observe. See if your perspective changes.

You might also miss many nuances if you skim or speed-read. The book contradicts the inattentive, fast pace of modern society. Use this book to help you slow down so you can begin to notice how God reveals Himself in the everyday.

Ultimately, we're called to redirect our attention away from the desires of the world and toward God. Whether we answer this call to come back home is up to us. If you're reading this far, know that you're one step closer to home. Someone has called you.

OPENING PRAYER

God, to whom all hearts are open, to whom everyone speaks their minds, and from whom nothing is hidden. I ask you to purify my heart's intentions with the indescribable gift of your grace so that I can love and praise you perfectly. Amen.

The opening prayer of The Cloud recognizes that our intentions might not be pure. Therefore, the prayer asks for God to purify the intentions. After all, if we have intentions based on our ego, which loves to be right, to win, or to gain, we might misconstrue The Cloud. The prayer also recognizes the all-knowing aspect of God. As much as we try to keep secrets from others—and ourselves—we can't keep them from God. Therefore, nothing is "new" for God.

PROLOGUE

In the name of the Father, the Son, and the Holy Spirit. I charge and entreat you, with as much strength and virtue as the bond of compassion allows, that if you own, keep, carry, or borrow this book, you will not read, write, speak, or let anyone else read, write, or speak it, unless it is to or for people with a sincere desire to follow Christ into contemplation. If someone reads, writes, talks, or hears it, you should charge him the same way I do: give him time to read, speak, write, or hear it again. If something isn't evident in the beginning or middle, it might make more sense later or at the end. If someone observed one thing but not another, he could be misled. Kindly do what I suggest to avoid this error in yourself and others.

I don't care whether fleshly babblers, self-blamers, gossips, tattletales, and cynics viewed this book. I don't want them or these curious, illiterate, or foolish men to get involved. They don't care, even if they're fine men with full lives. Men who live busy lives on the outside but are stirred on the inside by God's spirit would be soothed by God's grace if they could see it. They wouldn't notice it all the time like a contemplative person, but they'd see it at its peak.

This book has 75 chapters. The last chapter tells a person how to know if God has called him to this activity.

❖ ❖ ❖

The text opens with the Trinity—the Father, the Son, and the Holy Spirit, suggesting that the anonymous author is Catholic. He—and many scholars assume the author is male—stresses that the text should only be read by followers of Christ. The reader he has in mind is someone who has the desire to follow

Christ into the deepest depths of contemplation.

This also suggests that the reader already has an active faith practice. This helps possible misinterpretations of the text. He also suggests that you read the whole thing rather than skipping certain elements that might prove difficult.

This happens often in modern times, particularly in our spiritual practices. When things get difficult or even mundane, we skip over them to savor the juicy, sensory elements. This suggests having patience because things might not be clear at first, but over time, they will be clear.

We should take a holistic approach to The Cloud, which is the Catholic perspective on reading The Bible. Oftentimes, we'll rip off a quote from Scripture that might seem to suit our circumstance, but taken out of context, it might take on a different meaning. When we read the entire text and understand the entire meaning, we don't misinterpret certain elements if they are extracted.

The author knows that there will be people who will grab hold of the text and use it as "proof" of one thing or the other. There might even be some "experts" who don't understand the life of the contemplative and warn others of the dangers of contemplation.

He ends the prologue and begins the text by reminding readers to pay attention to where God is leading them. He knows that there will be skeptics and hypocrites who will challenge you on your path, but he reminds readers to keep their eyes on the prize.

CHAPTER 1

I see four levels and types of Christian men's lives, spiritual friend in God. Common, Special, Solitary, Perfect. Three can be started and finished in this life, and the fourth, with God's grace, will last forever in Heaven. As you can see, starting with "Common," then "Special," then "Solitary," and ending with "Perfect," I think that's how our Lord, out of His great mercy, called you and led you to Him by your heart's desire. You know that when you were living like most Christian men and hanging out with worldly friends, His love, which made and shaped you when you were nothing and bought you with His precious blood when you were lost in Adam, would not let you be so far away from Him in form and degree of living. So, He kindled your desire with great kindness, tied a leash of longing to it, and led you by it into a more special state and way of living, to be a servant among His special servants, where you could learn to live more spiritually in His service than in the ordinary way of living before.

He has loved you since you were a child, so He might not let you go so easily. But what did he do? Do you know how secretly and kindly He pulled you to the third degree and "Solitary" lifestyle? With the solitary life, you can raise the core of your being and move toward the perfect way of living.

He describes the Christian spiritual life as having four progressive phases—the *common*, the *special*, the *solitary*, and the *perfect*. Note that this assumes that one already has a grounded spiritual practice. The first three phases can be accomplished while we are alive, but he says we can get a glimpse of the fourth phase—the perfect—in this life. He suggests that the fourth phase never has a "completion" phase since it lasts unto eternity.

The *common* phase is where we might find many who attend church services regularly. It's "common" because you might have other friends with you in your spiritual community. It doesn't involve a special call, although many church groups will have "altar calls" where one professes Jesus as their personal Lord and Savior. This *common* phase is where many find joy in community participation. They actively worship and have great faith. There's nothing wrong with this faith, especially when it implores people to live in accord with spiritual principles.

However, God touches some hearts with a yearning for more. It's a desire that says the active, liturgical life isn't enough for them. They want to go deeper. It's not like they are bored with the community worship, but they know they want a closer relationship with God. The author calls this the *special* phase, where "you learned to live the interior life more perfectly than was possible in the common way[4]."

Still, yet, there is a burning desire to go deeper. By answering the call of this desire, we move to the *solitary*, which allows us to experience solitude. The active, community prayers are still intact, but we are further fed in the solitary practices. Eventually, we might be directed to the *perfect*.

CHAPTER 2

Now, broken one, look up. Why does God call you this? What a tired, sad, and sluggish heart, if not stirred by this love and this calling! Be careful with your enemy, broken one. Don't think you're better because you have a unique job and lifestyle. If you don't follow your calling with grace and advice, you'll be worse off and cursed. You should be so kind and loving to your spiritual spouse that God, King of Kings and Lord of Lords, would make Him low to you and choose you out of all His sheep as one of His special ones. Then He'd put you in pasture and feed you with His love as a preview of your inheritance, the Kingdom of Heaven.

Please fast. Now, forget the past. Don't focus on what you have. This is how to maintain gentleness. Spend your life longing to become perfect. God's power and your agreement should grant this wish. One thing, though. He's a jealous lover who won't share. Unless you're alone with him, he won't do what you want. He doesn't need anyone's help. Just look at Him and leave Him alone. Keep windows and doors of your senses shut to avoid flies and enemies. If you're willing to do this, humbly pray to him, and he'll help you soon. See how you fare. He's waiting and ready. Now what? What next?

This chapter isn't for the weary because it's about recognizing our place. So often pride disguises as piety and can interfere with our spiritual progress. Therefore, it's important to be humble the way Jesus was humble. Since Jesus chose you among his sheep, you can rest in a pasture to feed on God's love. Interestingly, this chapter contradicts modern writings that teach us to be grateful for what we have and live in the present. Although it tells us to look forward, not backward, it also tells us that our "whole life must be one of desire[5]," which contradicts some of the future chapters as well as some Zen teachings that tell us to be free from the pull of desire. However, this desire should be for God and God alone, which isn't spelled out here yet, but it will be later. This is why the author stresses for us to read the whole text—so that we don't take one chapter out of its context.

It is here we begin to see the parallels of the yoga limb of *pratyahara*, which is the withdrawing of the senses. It's also similar to St. John of the Cross' Night of the Sense. He instructs us to shut the door to our soul and stay within where God can do his work. What often happens is that our senses will beat on the door or try to sneak in through the window to pull us out of contemplation.

In his book, *Silence*, Thich Nhat Hanh also uses this window metaphor:

> *Our senses are our windows to the outside world. Many of us leave our windows open all the time, allowing the sights and sounds of the world to invade us, penetrate us, and compound the suffering in our sad, troubled selves.* [6]

Johnston's translation reads like this: "Close the doors and windows of your spirit against the onslaught of pests and foes, and prayerfully seek his strength[7]..."

CHAPTER 3

Raise your heart to God with love, and don't resent Him or His gifts. Look how reluctant He is to think about anyone else. Your mind and will should only serve Him. And forget all the creatures God has ever made and what they've done, so that neither your thoughts nor your desires are directed or stretched toward them, generally or specifically. Just ignore them. God loves soulwork most. Saints and angels are happy about this work and rush to help. All demons will be furious and try to stop you. You don't know how, but this work will help everyone on earth. Yes, this will help purgatory souls. By doing less, you clean up and simplify your life. When a soul is helped with grace, it's the easiest and fastest work. If not, it's difficult and wonderful.

Don't overwork. First, you see darkness. It's like a cloud is over your head, and you can only feel in your will that it's a pure intention to God. This darkness and cloud will always separate you from God. They prevent you from seeing Him clearly in your mind's understanding or heart's love.

Stay in the darkness as long as you can, calling for your loved one. If you ever feel or see Him, as you might here, stay in the cloud and darkness. If you work hard, God will let you succeed.

◆ ◆ ◆

Similar to the yoga teaching of dharana, we're called to fix our attention on God and God alone. Although in a worship or prayer practice we might have gratitude for the gifts God gives us, this is not the place to do that. This might be difficult at first, but the author tells us that the saints and angels will help us persevere.

This is also where those who aren't called to this practice might abandon it. Although this requires mental strength, we cannot do it by our own strength. We must be given this grace from God. He mentions that this also touches the souls of those in purgatory, and this begins to purify and strengthen our own spirit.

It is here we're introduced to the Cloud of Unknowing. Because we're often used to employing our imagination, or perhaps even our imagination will take us to beautiful places, we're called to abandon it. The Cloud of Unknowing is dark and lacks senses. All you have left is a "naked intent" to reach God. The author tells us this can be frustrating, but eventually we learn to endure it as our spirits become purified.

CHAPTER 4

I'll explain how it works so you don't misunderstand it.

Some think this work takes a long time, but it's the shortest possible. An atom is the smallest unit of time. It's so small it's hard to divide and understand. "For all the time you're given, you'll be asked how you used it" refers to this. And you should account for it, because it's neither longer nor shorter than your will. Because in an hour as many atoms can be in your will as wants or desires.

If you were changed by grace back to how your soul was before sin, you'd always be in control of that stirring. So no one strayed and everyone sought God, the most desirable thing. Because He is God, He fits our souls, and our souls fit Him because we were made in His image. And He alone is enough to satisfy our will and soul's desires. Because of this reforming grace, our soul can fully understand Him through love, something no created knowing power, such as an angel's or a person's soul, can do. Know, not love.

Hence the term "knowledgeable powers." All reasonable beings, including humans and angels, have a "knowledge power" and a "love power." God, who made the first knowing power, is hard to understand. God's second power, love, is easy to understand. A loving soul should be able to understand in itself that He is enough —and more, without comparison—to fill all souls and angels that will ever be. This is God's never-ending love miracle. See who by grace can see, because this feeling is endless happiness, not pain.

So, anyone who was changed by God's grace and stayed true to his will would never be without the endless sweetness in this life, nor would he have enough to eat in heaven. Don't be surprised if I tell you to work. This is the work man would have done if he hadn't sinned, as you'll hear later. This is the work for which man was made, and everything was made to help him. This work fixes men. Without contemplation, a person falls deeper into sin and farther from God. If a person only does this work, he or she gets farther from sin and closer to God.

Nothing is more valuable than time, so spend it wisely. Heaven could be won or lost so quickly. God never gives two times at once, proving time's value. He gives them sequentially. He does this because He won't change what He made. Time was made for us, not vice versa. God controls nature, so He won't delay the stirring of nature in a person's soul, which happens once. So people can't say, "You gave me two times at once, but I only had one stirring," when God asks how they spent their time at the end of the world.

You ask, "What should I do? How can I give a separate account of each time I've never paid attention to time until now? If I wanted to change it now, because of what you wrote before, it may not be natural or gracious for me to listen or make peace for more times to come. Yes, and I know from experience that I won't see anyone who comes after me because I'm too weak and my mind is too slow. These are the reasons, I'm sure. 'Jesus, I love you, help me!'"

You're right. Jesus will help if you love him. Love unites everything. Love Jesus, and you'll have everything He has. God creates time. Man keeps time. Because He's God and man, He's the best model for how to spend time. So, tie yourself to Him through love and faith, and you'll see things the same way He and others who love Him do. You'll be able to keep time like Our Lady Saint Mary, all the angels in heaven, and all the saints in heaven and on earth, who by Jesus' grace pay attention. Find out what it means and learn from it. I must warn you about one thing. Who could challenge Jesus, His righteous mother, His high angels, and His saints in this way? If he does, grace is helping him keep time so he can help the community, even if it's just a little.

So, pay attention to your heart's work. If it's really thought, it's a sudden movement that reaches God like a coal spark. It's amazing how much a willing soul can change in an hour. He may have forgotten everything in one move. Because of fleshly corruption, it quickly returns to a thought or deed done or undone. Why? Because it rises quickly as before.

These things aren't created by a humble and blind love, but by a proud, curious, and creative mind. If this work is to be done purely, a proud, curious mind must be crushed. Whoever reads or hears about this work and thinks it can or should be done through hard mental work, sits down and tries to figure it out, and in their curiosity works their mind against nature and pretends to work in a way that is neither physical nor supernatural, is dangerously fooled. Unless God, in His great goodness, shows him a miracle, makes him stop working, and leads him to the advice of people who have done it before, he will either go crazy or get caught up in spiritual sins and devils' tricks, which can cause him to lose his life and soul forever. Be careful with this work and don't use your imagination. Leave them alone; you can't get there by using them.

Don't assume that because I call it a darkness or a cloud it's an emotional cloud or when the lights are out in your house. You can imagine darkness and clouds on the sunniest summer day if you're clever. Imagine a bright light on a dark winter night. Not literal darkness. "Darkness" means "uncertainty." Your spiritual eye can't see what you don't know or have forgotten. Because it's between you and God, it's called a cloud of unknowing.

Although this text was written in the 15th Century, it touches on some of the problems of today—time, intellect, and imagination. We feel pressured to meditate for a specific time because we hear of others who can sit for that time. We also try to hasten how long it takes for us to "get there," in terms of how we will feel in the future once we've been able to sit for this period of time. The author said that this work can happen in an instant, but we often get in our own way.

What gets in our way? Among many things, our intellect and our imagination. These days, we often over-rationalize or overthink things. We try to reason our way to God. Think about a loving relationship with another—is it rational? I'm not talking about romantic relationships, although some might apply here. I can try to rationalize or reason why I love my dogs, but it makes no sense. I just love my dogs. I want to be with them. I talk to them and they respond not in words but in love. In the same way, we can't give evidence or reason why we're in a relationship with God. We can reason our love for God. We can't know and love him better through intellect. We know and love him through contemplation. Although we possess the power of the intellect and the power to love, the power of the intellect makes God difficult to comprehend. The power to love makes God comprehensible.

The other thing that gets in our way is our imagination. We try to pin an image of God in our minds or maybe stare at an image of Jesus to try to get us closer. That might help us at first, but we eventually must let that go. Our imaginings only get us so far, but then they get in the way. They keep us finite, whereas God is infinite.

The author also warns us to attend to the present moment. Think about it—God can't give two moments at once, but we often try to handle several moments at a time. Again, our intellect and our imagination will try to pull us towards the past or the future rather than bask in the present. He writes, "[I]n one tiny moment heaven may be gained or lost[8]." In other words, in each moment, there is heaven. Are we too fixed on what we have to do or what we want to occur so that we miss what's happening now?

During contemplation, we don't wish for a better past or agonize over the future. We just rest in this moment that God has given us.

CHAPTER 5

If you live and work on this cloud as I tell you, you must put a cloud of forgetting below you, between you and all future creatures, just as this cloud of unknowing is above you, between you and your God. You may feel far from God because of this cloud of unknowing. However, without a cloud of forgetting between you and all creatures, you're actually further from Him. When I say "all the creatures ever made," I include their actions and living conditions. I don't take out a single living thing or spirit, nor anything good or bad they've done or are doing. Everything should be forgotten.

Even though thinking about certain situations and special creatures can be helpful, it doesn't help in this work. why? When you remember or think about something God made or did, your soul's eye is opened to it and fixed on it, like a shooter's eye on the target. These thoughts still separate you from God. More thoughts about God's greatness create distance between you and God.

If it's polite and right to say so, it doesn't help much or at all to think about God's kindness or worthiness, Our Lady, the saints or angels in heaven, or even the joys in heaven, if you think this feeds your purpose. That won't help with this case or work. It's good to praise God for His kindness and love, but it's better to praise Him for who He is.

❖ ❖ ❖

During many prayer sessions, we seek answers. In fact, I remember Deepak Chopra suggesting that people ask a question before meditation, and the answer will arrive during the meditation session. Maybe.

If you look at the "eureka" moments that many people describe, they all have something in common. They become mired in solving a problem or finding the right word or idea. Sometimes the stress builds in their minds, which can frustrate this creative process. What often happens is the person walks away from the unsolvable and does something else, like go for a walk. It is then—when we abandon or surrender the unsolvable—that the solution arises.

This process is similar to the cloud of forgetting. The author suggests that we put everything, including thoughts of praise or images of God, into this cloud. He writes that although there is a cloud of unknowing that separates us from God, the true separation is our attachment to these ideas and imaginings.

If these clouds are difficult to imagine, here's another way of thinking about it. We often hear about the "mountaintop experience." Picture a mountaintop far off in the distance. You walk towards it, even though you don't know what the mountaintop looks like from up close. Still, you strive towards it. You don't need a map—your aim is fixed on the mountain.

What can pull you from your aim is if you stare at the map, or if you fixate on some berries or a mountain stream. Although the stream was formed by the mountain, walking towards the stream won't get you closer to the mountaintop. We also like to look behind us to see how far we've come. That also doesn't get us to the mountain. The cloud of forgetting is all of these things—even good things—that can distract us from the mountain. We fix our gaze on the mountain and just walk.

The author recognizes that there are times when we do need to check the map, be nourished by the berries, or be cleansed by the stream. We don't always practice contemplative prayer—at least at first. However, we try not to dwell on the taste of the berries, the coolness of the stream, or the different codes on the map while we're in contemplative prayer. The author writes, "For if your mind is cluttered with these concerns, there is no room for him."[9]

Therefore, when we're in contemplative practice, we don't

seek answers during the practice. Instead, we abandon the need to know.

CHAPTER 6

You ask, "How do I think about Him? Who is He?" I can only say "I dunno."

Because this question led me into the same darkness and cloud of unknowing as well. Because of God's grace, a person can understand all other living things and their works, but no one can understand God himself. I'd give up everything I can think of to love what I can't understand. Why? God should be loved, not deliberated. By love, but never by thought. Even though it's good to think about God's kindness and worthiness, it will be pushed down and forgotten in this work. You'll step over it bravely, but mischievously, with a sincere and pleasing love, and try to break through the darkness. Hit the thick cloud of unknowing with longing love and don't stop.

The author describes the Cloud of Unknowing as a darkness. It's dark because it has no known path. That's the point—abandoning what you know and moving forward. When many of us make a decision, we might have an initial preference, but then we ask several people what they think. The Cloud doesn't have any other decision aside from "forward," into the darkness, with no clue how long or how deep or how wide it is. The only "map" you have is your love for God.

That's the key—love for God. It's not to seek answers to problems or to gain power. It's about resting deep in love. It's like finding yourself in a semi-inflated parachute that envelops you in softness and holds you while you disappear from sight.

In today's culture, we believe that knowledge is power. That might be the case with worldly matters. But in spiritual matters, we venture into a different axis that goes beyond politics or even religious practices. It's beyond conservative or liberal. It's beyond race or culture. It's beyond sexuality or sexual preference or gender. It's beyond thought. It's just…beyond.

The author writes, "A man may know completely and ponder thoroughly every created thing and its works, yes, and God's works, too, but not God himself."[10] In a world that seek to covet things, ideas, and people, we don't seek to possess God. Instead, God possesses us.

We take these ideas of coveting and possessing and gain and tuck them away into the cloud of forgetting. We become more known when we drop what is known.

CHAPTER 7

If the darkness keeps asking what you want, say I only want God.

If this pesky thought asks, "What is that God," answer that God made, bought, and called you to your level. "You don't know Him," says the thought. Even if this thought seems holy and could help you find God, tell it to "go down again" and push it down with love. This thought may remind you of many good and wonderful things about God's kindness and that He is sweet, loving, gracious, and merciful. This thought doesn't want anything better. It will jangle until you think of His Passion.

This thought will show you how kind God is if you listen to it. Because it will soon show you how bad your old life was, and it may remind you of a place you used to live. So that when you die, you're scattered in unknown places. This scattering happened because you first listened on purpose, then answered, accepted, and left it.

The thought was good and holy. Yes, and so holy that a man or woman must first think about how bad they are, how kind people are, how good God is, and how worthy God is. They'll make a mistake and miss their goal if they don't. A person who has been doing these meditations for a long time should put them under the cloud of forgetting if they want to know God. When you decide to do this work and feel called by God's grace, lift your heart to God with love. Think of God as the one who made, bought, and called you to your degree. You can't list them all, though. Simply wanting to be close to God is enough.

Use a one-syllable word if you want to say something in one word to remember it better. The shorter something is, the better it fits the Spirit's work. Like GOD or LOVE. Look at the list and pick your favorite one-syllable word. Keep this word close so it never leaves you.

In peace or war, this word will be your sword and shield. This word will beat down clouds and darkness. This word can erase any thought. If your ego asks what you want, just say this word. If your ego mind offers to send a priest to explain the word, tell it, "You will have it whole, not broken or undone." Keeping your one-syllable word will keep your ego mind from consuming your desire for God.

The mind's incessant thought stream can be difficult to settle. In the same way, we're bombarded with messages from the media, similar messages can infiltrate our meditation because the mind is used to processing so much information at a time. We even hear messages that echo the many voices in society that challenge our belief in this God. These messages demand answers to this question: "Who is this God?" We might even be inclined to respond, but that only continues the conversation in our heads. It's almost like that Internet troll who challenges you, and as much as you try to respond, the troll is never satisfied. The troll continues to pick you apart, sending you into this never-ending rabbit hole that never leads to peace.

When we sit in prayer or meditation, the mind keeps spinning even when our bodies are still. The author advises us to tell these thoughts, "Be still." However, the mind might elicit a benevolent emotion, such as kindness, and then kind thoughts will follow. We might think that this is good—ruminating over kind thoughts. But this continues the mental chatter—the citta vrttis. This pulls us away from contemplation and towards more thoughts of "doing."

Similarly, we might find ourselves remembering our transgressions. This, too, might incline us to jump off our mat or cushion to make amends. The author says that it's important for us to remember these lapses in judgment to remind us that we're not perfect. If we don't realize that we need God for healing, we might easily be led to believe we don't need God at all. This can lead us down a dangerous, self-righteous road. However, thoughts of our sinfulness and feelings such as remorse should be tucked away in the cloud of forgetting while practicing contemplation. In other words, there's a time and place for contrition, and it's not during a contemplative prayer practice.

So how do we still our chattering minds? In the beginning, we use a short prayer word. The author suggests "God" or "love," preferring a single-syllable word. The key is to choose a word that is simple but doesn't cause you to generate more thoughts. You use this word to shield, not elaborate, excessive or obsessive thoughts.

When the chattering mind begins to ask questions, such as "What do you want?" We answer with this word, which will redirect our focus toward the Cloud of Unknowing. The word and our desire for God can penetrate this Cloud, where our hearts can pulse to God's rhythm.[11] The author here doesn't indicate whether this word is repeated continuously or only when thoughts arrive (which might be continuous).

Some yoga traditions espouse the use of a mantram specifically chosen by a student's guru. The student is told never to reveal this mantram to another to maintain its sanctity. These will typically be short phrases or words in Sanskrit. Eknath Easwaran advocates employing a mantram to help in meditation because it helps us "cross the sea of the mind."[12] He suggests using a short phrase in another language so that practitioners don't try to elaborate on the mantram. As The Cloud suggests, the mantram serves as a means of staving off distraction while walking closer to God. Over time, the mantram runs in the background of our minds while we carry out our daily activities. Then, when we have a moment of pause, the mantram can be heard.

This concept is similar to 1 Thessalonians 5:17, which tells us to "pray continually." Our lives can continually be directed towards God when we have a simple reminder processing in the background of our minds. It replaces concepts of greed or contempt. We see this in the 19th-century Russian story The

Way of a Pilgrim. The pilgrim repeats the phrase, "Lord Jesus Christ, have mercy on me, a sinner," hundreds of times a day, almost as an ascetic discipline. He learns, though, that this phrase becomes so ingrained in his mind that it repeats even when he consciously is not thinking about it. It automatically emerges when his mind becomes idle.

CHAPTER 8

You might ask, "Who is pushing me so hard, and is it good or bad? If it's bad, you wonder why it would increase a man's devotion if it's bad. Sometimes I find the stories comforting. For if they makes me cry, I think, sometimes because I feel sorry for Christ's suffering, sometimes because I feel sorry for myself, and for many other holy and helpful reasons. If he's good and makes me feel good with his sweet stories, I don't understand why you want me to push him into this cloud of forgetting."

This is a good question, so I'll try to answer it. First, if you ask me who is pressuring you to do this work and offering to help you. I'll tell you that it's your natural intelligence, written in your mind and soul. I'll tell you it's always good if you ask. It's a God-like beam. It's both good and bad. When God's grace opens it, you can see how bad you are, how much you care, how kind you are, and all the wonderful things God does in His living and dead creatures. It's not surprising, then, that it makes you more dedicated. The use is bad when priests and clerks are filled with pride and curiosity and want to be seen as proud scholars of the devil and masters of vanity and lies. In other people, religious or not, this natural mind is used in a bad way when it is filled with pride and curiosity about worldly things, as well as fleshly pride in wanting worldly worships, riches, and the false pleasures and flatteries of others.

If you ask me why you should forget it, it's because it's good by nature and when used well, it makes your devotion grow. There are two ways to live in the Holy Church, I say. First, an active life, then a contemplative one. The active life is at the bottom, and the contemplative life is at the top. The active and contemplative lives have high and low points. Even though they're different, neither can be lived fully without the other. Why? The most important part of an active life is less important in a contemplative life. Man can't be fully active without being partly contemplative, and vice versa. Active lives begin and end in this life, but contemplative lives begin now and last forever. Why? Mary of Bethany's choice will always be with her. Active life has many worries, but contemplative life finds peace with one thing.

Kindness and charity are part of being active. The higher part of an active life and the lower part of a contemplative life lie in good spiritual meditations and being busy looking at one's own misery with sorrow and repentance, at Christ's suffering and His followers with pity and compassion, and at the wonderful gifts, kindnesses, and works of God in all of His living and dead creatures with thanks and praise. The higher part of contemplation, as it can be had here, hangs in this darkness and cloud of unknowing, with a loving stirring and a blind looking only at God Himself.

At the bottom of his active life, a man is below himself. In the higher parts of an active and contemplative life, a man is with himself. At the highest level of contemplation, a person is above himself and below God. Above himself because he wants to get there by grace, not by his works. He's spiritually connected to God and wants the same things. A person can't get to the higher part of active life without stopping the lower part, and the same is true for contemplative life. Meditating on the holy things he does can interfere with contemplation just as working with a false stirring of love that might come between him and God.

I tell you to forget a sharp, subtle thought, even if it's holy and promises to help you reach your goal. We don't know why love could reach God in this life. So long as the soul is in this dead body, our understanding is sharp when spiritual things, especially God, are mixed with fantasy. We'd be dirty otherwise. Without wonder, we'd be led astray.

◆ ◆ ◆

It's cumbersome to try to determine whether or not our

thoughts are "good" or "evil." We can wrack our brains for a long time trying to discern the nature of these thoughts. Even simple thoughts like "freedom" can pull us towards evil, especially when our freedom encroaches on the rights or safety of others. Although our thoughts about God's grace or kindness can warm our hearts and strengthen our resolve, pride will sometimes infiltrate these thoughts.

This is when we begin to have ideas of "favor"—that God somehow prefers us over others. We even see this with the Pharisee, who praises his own righteousness and thanks God that he's not a sinner like the tax collector. Although the Pharisee might have been well-versed in God's law, pride can corrupt the intellect. We might see this today when the religious get too concerned with worldly affairs or align themselves with politics. Pride fuels the desire for power. Therefore, the author tells us to abandon all of these thoughts—"good" and "bad"—into the cloud of forgetting.

He also explains that there's an appropriate time to concern ourselves with things of the world and thoughts about God. He describes two "lives" in the Church—the active and the contemplative. Although he doesn't specify whether these lives are phases to move through or times throughout the day, he does indicate that these lives are somewhat interdependent. Within both of these lives are the lower and higher parts.

The lower active life is more outward-facing. These are acts of service not only towards others but also observances and disciplines to strengthen our faith and align our purpose to God. In the yoga tradition, we can see these as the yamas and the niyamas—the first two branches of ashtanga yoga—that help to get our outside lives in order so that we can begin to cultivate our inner life. We might also consider the active asana practice—at first—to be the lower active life.

Here's where it gets confusing, but it also points to the interdependence of the active and the contemplative lives. The higher active is the same as the lower contemplative. In other words, lives merge at this stage. This is when we begin to look within. We begin welcoming the internal dialogue while relying less on the outward expressions of our faith. If we compare this to the yoga tradition, we begin to integrate our physical asana practice with what's going on in our minds. We begin to tune into the breath through pranayama. Although these are still outward-facing, they help us tune within.

Eventually, we might move to the higher contemplative stage. It is here that our intellect serves no purpose. If we find ourselves in this Cloud of Unknowing, we don't concern ourselves with whether we should rather be feeding the poor. We know we have to lay that active part aside. By thinking, we might distract ourselves away from the presence of God.

The author writes that we might experience this higher contemplative stage during our lives, but it's mostly experienced after passing through this life.

CHAPTER 9

These stirring thoughts, which will always press on you when doing this work, must always be controlled. If you don't, they will control you so much so that when you think it's best to stay in the darkness and think only of God, you'll see that your mind is on something below God. If so, it's between you and God for now. So, empty your mind of clear insights, no matter how holy or likely. It is better for your soul and more pleasing to God to persist in a blind stirring of love to God for Himself and an awareness pressing on this cloud of unknowing than to bask in the wild imaginings of angels and saints in heaven.

If you could see it as clearly as you can by God's grace and grasp and feel it in this life, you'd agree. People won't see clearly in this life. God's grace gives people that feeling. So send love to the cloud. Let God draw your love to that cloud and try to forget everything else with His grace.

Since a simple mind of something under God that pushes you away from Him makes it harder to feel His love, what makes you think a memory you want to remember won't get in the way of your plans? If thinking about a saint or a clean spirit slows you down so much, what makes you think thinking about a miserable person or anything physical or worldly will slow you down less and let you do this work?

I'm not saying it's bad if a good, clean spiritual thing under God competes with your blind desire for God or inspires you to be more dedicated to this work. No way! Even though it's good and holy, it hurts more than it helps because it demands your attention. Perfectly seeking God won't find peace in angels or saints in heaven.

◆ ◆ ◆

The second verse of the Yoga Sutras of Patanjali states that the goal or purpose of yoga is to cease the internal chattering of the mind. We all experience this, particularly if we're not engaged in problems solving or other tasks that demand our concentration. When we sit alone with nothing to do, our minds begin to ruminate over the past, anticipate the future, or obsess over our emotional states. When we pray or meditate, the chatter might escalate, depending on the subjective urgency of the issues of our past, present, or future.

The author tells us that all of these thoughts interfere with experiencing God. Our thoughts are placed above us between us and God. Although thoughts of God aren't necessarily bad, they can easily pull us away from our blind desire for God alone. He describes the cloud as a darkness void of any imaginings. It's here we see a contrast between Ignatian Contemplation,[13] which emphasizes imagination based on scripture reading, and this type of contemplation, which is about emptying.

We also see echoes of 1 Corinthians 13:15: "For now we see only a reflection as in a mirror; then we shall see face to face. Now I know in part; then I shall know fully, even as I am fully known."

The author reiterates that we might have a glimpse of the higher form of contemplation in this life, but it will be fully experienced after we die. So how do we get our minds to stop thinking? This might be impossible for us. If we have the desire to experience God, God will teach us.

CHAPTER 10

This isn't about a memory of a person or body in this world. A sudden, bare thought of any of them easily presses against your will and mind. Yet if this sudden stirring or thought is not put out quickly, your fleshly heart can easily lead you astray with some kind of liking if it pleases you or has pleased you. This fasting can be torture for people who are easily distracted by the worldly temptations, but it is not torture for you and all others who have truly left the world and who will be ruled not by their own will and minds, but by the will and counsel of their sovereigns, whether religious or secular. You put your trust in God from the start of your life, with testimony and advice from a wise counselor.

If you let this liking or grumbling stay in your fleshly heart for too long, it will stick to your spirit heart with your consent. These thoughts can become sins. This is what happens when you or the people I'm referring to remind you of a living person or physical object. Wrath is anger and a desire for revenge. A deep dislike and contemptuous way of acting toward them, along with bad thoughts is envy. A feeling of being tired and not wanting to do anything good is called sloth.

If something makes you happy or has in the past, thinking about it can make you happy to the extent you attach your heart to it. This means you want nothing but peace and quiet with whatever you're thinking about. If a thought you have or accept is worthy of nature, knowing, grace, degree, favor, or fair-mindedness, it is Pride. It's covetous to want someone else's money, possessions, or other resources. Gluttony is enjoying tasty meats, drinks, or other pleasures. If it's love, pleasure, or fleshly flirting, gloating, or flattering, it's lust.

◆ ◆ ◆

When we sit in meditation, some thoughts that arise stem from the seven deadly sins: anger, gluttony, sloth, pride, lust, envy, and greed. Having thoughts is not a sin, but when the thoughts begin to stir one of these vices, it can become a problem. These vices can easily drive us towards conflict with ourselves and others, and they come between us and God.

These vices have energies of their own—passion—that drive us towards action. Sitting with these kinds of thoughts and letting them have their way with us can lead us away from contemplation. They pull us off our mat—or, as Desert Father Evagrius suggested, force monks from their cell of solitude.

Although passion today is often seen as a "good" motivator that helps us accomplish our goals, it wasn't always the case[14]. The Latin root of passion is *pati* or *patior*, which means "to suffer." If you think about Christ's passion, it was suffering—something done to him. Passion, therefore, was an energy that drove you into some sort of suffering. It can make some sense today when we voluntarily suffer to achieve a certain goal.

We might feel like we're driven by passion to achieve something or acquire something, but if you go back to the seven deadly sins, how might these drive your intentions? In other words, we might feel passionate to achieve career goals, but does this point to our greed, gluttony, or pride? How often do we feel attracted to someone—we call it "passion"—but it's actually our lust taking control of us? Even today, we often think lust is healthy in a relationship, but over time, it might mask our ability to see the other person more clearly.

Altogether, these energies—these "passions"—can drive us towards pain. We might find them scintillating at first, but ultimately, they serve to drive us away from God.

CHAPTER 11

I don't say this because I want you or others like you to sin, but because I want you to weigh every thought and movement and work hard to destroy the first movement and thought of these things that could make you sin. Anyone who doesn't consider their first thought, even if it's not a sin, will be careless in small sins. In this dangerous world, no one can completely avoid sin, but perfectionists should never commit trivial sins. If they don't, I'm not surprised they sin dangerously.

◆ ◆ ◆

We often talk about the effect of so much media distracting our ability to think, but even in the 16th century, people were still troubled by incessant thoughts. Although our thoughts today can often stem from interactions or instant messages from around the globe, some of those thoughts are reactions to what we see around us. For example, we might be watching a movie, but our thoughts are sometimes bouncing between the plot itself and our feelings about the actor's ability. Some former social media influencers recall living their lives thinking about their next post and subsequent hashtag to grow their following. Even when we look at something beautiful such as a sunrise or sunset, we comment on its beauty and perhaps compare it to others we've seen before.

The author writes that we need to investigate our thoughts. He doesn't say, though, when we should do this, particularly since he says in other chapters that as soon as a thought arises, we beat it with our sacred word into the cloud of forgetting.

Some meditation instructors such as Tara Brach tell us to welcome each thought—good or bad—and accept it without attaching too much significance to it. This might keep us in a continual state of judging our thoughts to the point that we might never rest. Other instructors will tell us to acknowledge each thought but don't grasp it. They compare thoughts to trains coming into a station—and you don't jump onto the train (of thought) that can take you in an undesired direction. And still, other instructors will suggest attending to the thoughts the way you might attend to a movie you've seen a million times before—you don't pay much attention to it, but just watch the stream passively without engaging it. The movie is still playing, but you're fixed on something beyond the screen. These mental games can be challenging and might pull us off the meditation cushion. It's no wonder people might find meditation and prayer difficult. No one said it's easy, even though it's relatively simple.

What might be helpful is if we take the author's advice for examining your thoughts AFTER contemplation. This is an inquiry into how easily your thoughts can steer you off course. This requires certain backtracking, and it, too, can become a practice in itself. It might be easier if you do this alone without distractions. After taking a deep breath, you sigh and wait for the next thought to arrive. Once it does, stay with it and wonder where it came from. Was it something from the immediate environment? Was it something that's pressing on your current schedule? Was it a physical discomfort or sensation that gave rise to a thought? Each thought has an origin. Typically it stems from something that has happened recently or something that is continually setting you off. In cognitive psychology, we call this temporal accessibility and chronic accessibility.

Once you become aware of how thoughts arise, you then see how some thoughts might be hijacking your contemplative practice. Is there a thought of guilt? Do you feel uncomfortable about not "doing it right?" Is a particular emotion weighing heavily on you now that colors your practice? Usually, emotions give birth to thoughts.

What the author is particularly concerned about is how our thoughts might lead us to sin. You might consider the last thing you did that resulted in your suffering. It might be something trivial, such as overindulging in food or drink that led you to be sick. Or it could be something more profound, such as cheating on your taxes or your partner. These actions were a result of a mix of emotion and thought that snowballed because we lacked awareness or discernment. We became careless and impulsive with our thinking, and we didn't pay careful attention to how our emotions will get into the driver's seat of our thoughts and subsequent actions.

The more we tend to our thoughts in this time of self-reflection, the more we can get out of impulsive and compulsive behaviors. Then, we spend less time trying to settle our roller coaster of drama while in contemplation. We have less to process and more to rest.

CHAPTER 12

Don't give up if you want to succeed. Keep beating this cloud of unknowing between you and God with longing love. Don't think about God or anything that happens. This work destroys sin's ground and root. You've never fasted, slept, risen, or worked so hard. Even if you could cut out your eyes, pull out your tongue, stop your ears and nose, and torture your body—none of this would help. You'll still sin.

Don't cry over your sins or Christ's death, and don't dwell on heaven's joys. What will this do? It could bring good, help, money, and grace, but it does or could do little without this blind love stirring. This is Mary of Bethany's best feature. Without this love, they lose. It destroys the root of sin and brings virtues with it. If it's really thought of, all virtues will be perfectly thought of and felt in it, without any mixing of intent. A man can have as many virtues as he wants, but without this blind love, all of his virtues are mixed with bad intentions and aren't as good.

Virtue is planned and measured love aimed at God for God. why? He causes all virtues. If someone does a good thing for reasons other than God, even if God is the main cause, it's not as good as it could be. One or two virtues instead of all can illustrate this. Meekness and kindness are needed. Whoever understands these two things has everything.

◆ ◆ ◆

I find it fascinating to learn about some of the ascetic practices from various traditions. Some will hold their breath for minutes on end while sitting nearly naked in subzero temperatures. Others will tighten a belt around their leg that digs deep into the skin. Some will drink only water for weeks or self-flagellate with a thorny whip. These ascetic practices are meant to detach from sinful desires and purify the self. If a man is tempted by pornography, would gouging out the eyes alleviate this temptation? The temptation still exists deep in the mind and will find other ways to entice the soul. Ascetic practices serve as punishment for unhealthy behaviors or thoughts, but they do little to remove the desire, which is the seed of the behavior or thought.

Granted, discipline is important. Oftentimes we allow our indulgences to take over, particularly on vacation or during holidays, and we must redirect ourselves towards more healthy behaviors. We learn, through experience, that when we let our desires run the show, we're never satisfied. We might think that one piece of cake isn't harmful, but we eventually let our guard down to overindulgence. Addictions rarely start with indulgence—it's a gradual tearing of willpower.

Although guilt can weigh heavily on our spirit, a healthy dose of it plays a role in setting us on a more noble path. We might feel guilty for letting our anger overcome us, but then we repent —we decide that we will try to do better next time. A healthy dose of guilt can also build our humility—knowing that we're not perfect and we make mistakes just like everyone else. Guilt can also build empathy and forgiveness—we don't judge others for their mistakes and we forgive them the way we desire to be forgiven.

The author mentions that these acetic practices and feeling guilt have their place, but contemplative work is paramount. Contemplation pulls the weed of sin from its root rather than allowing it to grow again. In its place, contemplation grows virtue.

Many people can have virtues, but they can easily be tainted by selfish intentions. In other words, the love for God can be virtuous, but the desire to possess God for oneself can build walls between people. We might be charitable, but if it's mixed with pride or the need for approval, then it isn't perfect. The author says that virtues are purified in contemplation because they are authentic. We then respond to every situation without selfish intentions.

CHAPTER 13

First, let's look at humility and how it's not perfect when it's not caused by God, even though God is most important. God-caused humility is perfect. First, let's look at what humility is in and of itself, and then what causes it.

Imperfect humility is knowing and feeling who you are. Anyone who knows himself should be humble. Two things create humility. One is man's filth, misery, and weakness due to sin, which he will always feel as long as he lives in this world, no matter how holy he is. God's love and worthiness make nature shake, clerics look foolish, and saints and angels look blind. I can't say what would have happened if He hadn't used His divine wisdom to judge their sight based on nature and grace.

This second way—perfect humility—is eternal. The other way is imperfect because it will not only fail at the end of this life, but it can also cause a soul in this mortal body to lose and forget everything he knows and feels about himself, no matter how good or bad he was in this life. Whether a soul like this experiences this perfect humility often or rarely, I think it's brief. During this time, the soul knows and feels only God. And when it knows and feels the other's cause and talks with them about it, it's not perfect humility. Even so, imperfect humility is still good and necessary.

◆ ◆ ◆

Humility is a well-known virtue, but it's often suffocated in self-love and "It's not your fault" movements. Indeed, sufferers of abuse and trauma swing way off into victimhood, blaming themselves for episodes and life stages where others are responsible. On the other hand, pride can easily disguise itself as empowerment where little responsibility is assumed for past mistakes. Pride makes excuses rather than confessions. Our current concept of humility is rooted in the idea that no matter our accomplishments, we are no better than others in God's eyes. We recognize how many shoulders we stand on when receiving any reward, but we also hoist others onto our shoulders.

Humility is the acceptance of who we are without regard for status or past action. It's starting each moment new again with an open hand to receive God's gifts. It is taking responsibility for our actions in this moment and taking nothing for granted. We don't feel we deserve anything, so entitlement is eschewed. As noble as humility might be, the author calls this "imperfect humility" because it is finite—tied to our current life. It is imperfect because there might be moments where pride might swoop in and tempt us into believing we are more than we are.

Mind you, this idea stems from the Christian perspective of Original Sin, where Adam and Eve ate from the Tree of Knowledge and defied God. This perspective assumes that all of us inherit this "stain" of sin, so without the salvation of God, we are all born "wretched."

However, even the most chaste and holy of people might have moments of forgetting God. Those moments when we do not have God on our mind can be turned towards a sinful thought or behavior. Because we have those moments, though brief, any humility stemming from mankind is considered "imperfect."

On the other hand, humility originating from God is considered to be "perfect" because it's eternal. It's always flowing. It is the "superabundant love and worthiness of God himself, before whom all of nature quakes, all scholars are fools, and all saints and angels are blind."[15] We might experience this perfect humility for a brief moment, where we forget our individual self and become immersed in God. This brief glimpse of perfect humility is not ours to keep, but it serves as a beacon for what's to come.

The author clarifies that imperfect humility is still a virtue to cultivate in this lifetime.

CHAPTER 14

Despite calling it "imperfect humility," I'd rather know who I am than have all the saints, angels, and members of the Holy Church, religious or not, pray for me. Sinners can't get or keep perfect humility.

Work hard to know yourself as you are. Then, you'll understand and feel God as He is, I predict. Not as He is in Himself, as only He can, and not as you will in bliss with your body and soul. As He allows, a gentle soul can live in this temporal body.

Because I listed two types of humility, one perfect and one imperfect, don't think I want you to stop being imperfectly humble and focus on being perfect. No, you shouldn't do that. I do what I do to show you how important this spiritual exercise is before any other spiritual or physical exercise a man can do by grace. How a secret love pressed in purity of spirit on this dark cloud of unknowing between you and your God perfectly contains humility without any special or clear seeing under God. Because I wanted you to know what perfect humility was, you did it for us both. Because it will make you kinder.

Because I think ignorance leads to pride. If you didn't know what perfect humility was, you might think your imperfect humility was the perfect type. You were full of foul, stinking pride and mistook it for humility. Work hard to achieve perfect humility, because whoever has it won't sin for a long time.

◆ ◆ ◆

Self-knowledge is an important component of humility—both perfect and imperfect. It's the ability to recognize how our past conditioning can shape how we perceive the world and ourselves. It's shaving off some of the false layers of pride that mask our ability to know our role in our past, current, and future circumstances. We take responsibility for ourselves when we know ourselves. Once we begin to understand ourselves, we might catch a glimpse of experiential knowledge of God. However, this self-knowledge doesn't come easy. Humility wipes away the soot of our false selves and we are left looking clearly at ourselves. We realize that there have been moments where we've been wrong. We see how our pride might have denied or rationalized our bad behavior. By recognizing our mistakes and owning up to them, we lay new tracks onto a different path. This is at the heart of repentance—the turning away from ways that brought harm to ourselves or others. We see how our behavior put a barrier between us and God, and we begin to chip away at this barrier.

Some spiritual traditions want to bypass this step. Sure, we might heed an altar call and dunk our heads in cold water to begin anew. That might free us from divine punishment, but it doesn't rid us of the urge to sin. Once we recognize the patterns that got us there, we have to remove those patterns and behaviors. We have to make amends.

Although the contemplative path seems free from this work of self-knowledge—that we can just engage in contemplative prayer without self-awareness—this, too, is bypassing. The author writes that we must pass through imperfect humility before we can even step into the realm of perfect humility. He writes, "Indeed, it is impossible for a sinner to get hold of and retain perfect humility without imperfect humility."[16]

This is why major religions are losing. The spiritual traditions promise that self-knowledge isn't necessary since we are changing all of the time. Because what's most important is the present moment (which, in most instances, it is), they claim that we shouldn't live in the past. For those far along the spiritual journey, this is the case. However, for those just beginning, this leads novices to believe they can bypass the dirty work.

Even Buddhist monk Pema Chodron said, "Dried shit on the wall doesn't stink." In other words, we can easily ignore the conditioning (the shit) of our past, but it will still prevent us from seeing clearly. So imperfect humility compels us to get a good whiff of ourselves. We must go through this process.

Some even believe they've had a glimpse of God, thinking they've been "enlightened." They think this path can easily be skipped if you tap here or change the chemistry of your genes. That's pride deluding people into thinking they've achieved perfect humility because they've achieved a little bit of self-knowledge. It takes time and effort for spiritual maturity, and we might never know if we've ever "reached" maturity, let alone perfect humility. The author writes that "[p]erfect humility is not a destination. Those who believed that they've 'arrived' have merely found another way to wrap themselves in filthy, stinking pride."[17]

However, if we set our minds toward God without needing to achieve anything but God, our actions will eventually navigate toward God. Think about it—if you truly loved someone, you would do what is necessary to please that person. In the same way, we bend our will towards God and become less inclined towards sinful behaviors.

CHAPTER 15

You can reach perfect humility through grace in this life. I say this to prove that they are mistaken when they suggest that being reminded of how horrible we are and have been is the best way to be humble.

I believe that for those who are used to sinning, like I am and have been, the fastest way to change is to be humbled by remembering our sorrow and sins we've already committed, until the great rust of sin is mostly gone, as our conscience and counsel attest. Some who are "innocent" because they were weak and didn't know better can be called by God to be contemplatives. Even us, if our counsel and conscience testify to our lawful repentance in contrition, confession, and penance according to all-Holy Church's law and ordinance—there is another cause to be humbled. Our Lady Saint Mary's life is above that of the most sinful penitent in Holy Church, and Christ's life is above that of any man in this life or an angel in paradise, who has never felt weakness and never will. These are above a weak man's life.

If the only perfect reason to be humble is to see and feel remorse, then I'd ask individuals who say that why they should be humble if they've never felt remorse of wrongdoing and never will. This is the case for Jesus, Mary, and all the saints and angels in heaven, who are perfect. The gospel calls us to this and all other perfections. He tells us to be as flawless as He is by grace.

◆ ◆ ◆

The author continues his discourse on humility, arguing that if humility only meant recognizing our sinfulness, then Jesus and the Blessed Mother wouldn't have perfect humility. Here's what I find to be interesting—he writes that those who continue to sin need to reflect on these sins. In other words, we can't have it both ways—we can't maintain a hedonist mentality and be able to experience perfect humility, let alone enlightenment. This is where so much excusing occurs, and this is where we fall into the trap of "spiritual, but not religious." We want the feel-good aspect of spirituality without discipline.

However, this discipline is necessary. When we begin a meditation practice, we find it difficult to sit for just a minute, let alone 20 minutes. It becomes intolerable. Our minds begin to process and churn all the events that have occurred or will occur and the emotions bookmark things by repeating them. So what do we do? We tell ourselves that we can't meditate. We say, "That's just not my personality" or "It's not possible for people to do that."

If that's the case, how do you explain the many Buddhists who can sit for hours in meditation? Do you think that just happened overnight—that they one day decided to become a Buddhist and sit for an hour in meditation? Those monks who live deep in Tibet practice tummo[18] to keep warm—that's not done without practice.

Therefore, we have to abide by certain disciplines to keep us centered. The Hebrew word for "sin" is hhata, which means "miss the mark." Whether it's accidental (from ignorance) or deliberate (from our free will), we often make choices that stray us from the path. In the Buddhist Eightfold Path,[19] adopt the ethical practices of right speech, right action, and right livelihood. In the Yoga Sutras, we employ the yamas, which are concerned with how we behave in the world, and the niyamas, which describe how we develop ourselves.

These practices from the Eastern tradition keep us on the mark. It doesn't mean that we don't stray every once in a while, but we abide by them to grow closer to our goal, whether it's God, enlightenment, or unity.

Many yoga teachers criticize those who parallel the Ten

Commandments with the Yamas and niyamas, but I'm not one of them. Indeed, although the Judeo-Christian tradition teaches that the breaking of these commandments condemns you, the Yoga Sutras and Buddhist teachings will say that too much straying from the path won't get you to the summit. These disciplines serve as guideposts along the way. The path might be steep in certain places, particularly if you're previous practices weakened you, but they keep you ascending.

Through time, practice, and discipline, you'll find that meditation comes easier. The mind isn't processing any more drama because off the mat or cushion, you're less inclined to create more. Once you've had a peek at the summit, the author says (in Chapter 14) that you won't want to sin.

CHAPTER 16

Watch that no one thinks it's arrogant for the worst sinner in this life to take him on after he's been legally forgiven and after he's felt drawn to the contemplative life by his counsel and conscience, to offer a humble stirring of love to his God, pressing on the cloud of unknowing between him and his God. Jesus' words to Mary of Bethany apply to all contemplative sinners. Not because she was sad, remembered her sins, or was humbled by the situation. Why? She loved deeply.

Here, people can see what a secret act of love can buy from our Lord. Despite her sins, she was sad and cried a lot. Because of her hardships, she was humble. So should we, as sinners. Because of how bad we've been, we should feel terrible sorrow for our sins forever and be humble.

Mary did. Even though she didn't feel the pain of her sins, she carried them like a burden in her heart. She felt sad and resolute that she was the worst kind of wretch and that her sins had separated her from the God she loved. They contributed to her illness and death because she lacked love. Why? So, did she descend from the height of her desires to the depths of her sinful life, searching in the foul, stinking dunghill of her sins and crying over each one individually? No way. Why? She knew she couldn't do it because God's grace gave her wisdom. She may have been more likely to sin often than to buy forgiveness with that work.

So, she put her love and longing in this cloud of unknowing and learned to love something she couldn't see clearly in this life, either with the light of understanding or the sweetness of love. She couldn't remember if she'd done anything wrong. Yes, and I hope she loved His divinity so much that she didn't notice His beautiful body as He spoke and preached in front of her, or anything else, living or dead. The Bible says so.

◆ ◆ ◆

One figure in the Bible that has caused so much confusion and controversy is Mary Magdalene. For so many years, she was considered a prostitute, mostly because Pope Gregory I of Magdala, Mary of Bethany, and the "sinful woman with the alabaster jar." We see this tradition in Chapter 15 of The Cloud, where the author mentions the passage from Luke 7:48 ("your sins are forgiven") yet also mentions "Mary." The discourse discusses at length this woman's pain for her sins but recognized her as a contemplative because her love for Jesus was so strong. Rather than weep excessively for her sins, which would keep her deep in rumination to the point of losing hope for forgiveness, she would weep for her forgetting about God's love. She recognized that while she was committing her sins, she was not loving God. That was what pained her the most, the author writes, but because "she loved much," her sins were forgiven.

Although the Gallacher, Johnston, and Underhill texts only refer to her as "Mary" but do not distinguish which Mary, the Billy translation specifies this figure to be Mary Magdalene[20]. The Butcher text also specifies this as Mary Magdalene and alludes to a possible relationship with Jesus. This, of course, fuels the popular controversy that Mary Magdalene and Jesus were married and had a child together. Logically, this makes little sense because it would indicate that Mary would have either been pregnant or given birth to this child before his crucifixion. Further, the gospel of Mary Magdalene doesn't refer to a child, even if the first few pages of that gospel remain missing.

Even though Mary Magdalene has been deemed the first contemplative (others would say it's the Blessed Mother), the extensive discourse regarding her sins in this chapter indicates another woman, such as the woman with the alabaster jar.

Mary of Magdala, according to Luke 8:2, only said to be healed of seven demons. Rather than being sinful, it's been recognized that those who were possessed by demons actually suffered from a mental disorder, such as epilepsy or schizophrenia. Some modern movies portray Mary Magdalene as suffering from mental illness as a result of her being raped by Roman soldiers[21]. Although there is no evidence of this, it does suggest that Mary of Magdala wasn't the woman so caught up in her sins as a result of her behavior.

CHAPTER 17

Mary sat at Jesus' feet while Martha prepared His food, according to the Gospel of Luke. When she heard His words, she didn't look at her sister's good and holy work, because that's part of active life. She didn't look at His blessed body or the sweetness of His voice and words, even though they were better and holier, because that's the second part of active life and first part of contemplative life.

But His humanity's dark words lapped against His Godhood's wisdom, and she loved Him. No matter what she saw, heard, or did, she wouldn't leave. Instead, she sat still in her body with many sweet privies and slow love between her and God. There has never been a pure creature in this life who was so enamored with thinking about and loving God that there wasn't a cloud of unknowing between them.

Mary felt pure love. Why? She didn't want to lose the best and holiest contemplation in this life. When her sister Martha complained about her to Jesus and asked Him to tell her to help her, Mary just sat there and didn't say or do anything to make her sister think she was wrong. She had another job Martha didn't know about. She couldn't listen to or comfort her when she cried.

All of Jesus' actions, words, and gestures with these two sisters should be a model for all active and contemplative Christians from then until the end of time. All contemplatives should follow Mary's example. All actives should model Martha.

❖ ❖ ❖

How many of us say, "I just don't have time"? For myself, I will sigh at my cluttered apartment, frustrated that I "don't have time" to empty the dishwasher or even get rid of the odds and ends on my dining room table. Yet I seem to log 3-4 hours a day on my phone reading the latest bullshit on Donald Trump or watching old Mean Tweets on Jimmy Kimmel's YouTube channel. Even now, I had realized that my watch's battery is low, so I tried to find the charger all over my cluttered apartment, complaining about how I can't find anything in this 800-square-foot space. I return to my computer, only to find I left my glasses…somewhere.

That took more than five minutes of my life. I've been up since 4:45, and I'm just getting to writing now that it's after 7:00. Where does the time go?

I was reminded of this early this morning, and I kept searching and searching for the Blaise Pascal quote about time. I Googled it, tried to search for it on the online version of Pensees, and even looked through one of my old posts on Medium about it. Then, I realized that I had spelled "Pascal" incorrectly, and my type-A personality needed to fix it. So as I was fixing and republishing, I noticed a good article on Medium about the importance of God, so of course, I wanted to read and craft an intelligent response. Then I noticed a comment on one of my latest posts on Medium, so I had to respond to that.

Hmm…and I wonder where my time goes.

All that time searching for that Pascal quote—I realized it was from Seneca. Not French, but Greek. Not 1669, but 49 A.D. Here are the wise words about time from Seneca:

> *It is not that we have a short time to live, but that we waste a lot of it. Life is long enough, and a sufficiently generous amount has been given to us for the highest achievements if it were all well invested. But when it is wasted in heedless luxury and spent on no good activity, we are forced at last by death's final constraint to realize that it has passed away before we knew it was passing.[22]*

Yep, that pretty much sums it up.

Matthew 6:21 says, "Wherever your treasure is, there the desires of your heart be." We can think of time as a treasure, even if some confusing New Age people will say bullshit like, "Time is only an illusion" or "Time is just a story." Please.

How we spend our time is a good indicator of what's important to us. We might even know that other things are important, but how we spend our time reveals to us what our priorities—or our "true" desires are. It also shows what's not important to us.

It takes a bit of reflection to reveal what these are. Let's take my morning, for example. My apartment is excessively cluttered. That, in itself, is revelatory because it reflects my cluttered head. I've been praying for years—yes, YEARS—for clarity. How can clarity come when I don't even have it in my own apartment?

It takes time to de-clutter, and yet I tell myself I don't have it. Actually, I do, but when I make time, I'm too exhausted. It shows that I don't have "clarity" as my priority.

So what IS my priority? For most of my life, I've been excessively curious. This can be a burden because my curiosity often drives me down a rabbit hole of obsessiveness. It's shown itself in my desire to know more about a guy I like, or a desire to find out who wrote that quote about time. That natural curiosity, almost to the point of neurosis, can serve as my focus and drive me toward the goal I want to achieve.

I can continue to peel that back, wondering why I'm so curious. What is it I'm really seeking? Perhaps it's a deep-seated desire for power—to know more than others. Or it could be a desire to win—in case I'm in an argument about Greek philosophy and time (I know, I'll lose that one badly).

I can ask myself, "Is this the best use of my time?" Seneca might disagree because it's not being spent on my "highest achievement." If my desire to know—my curiosity—can be used for trifle things, then certainly it can be retooled for my writing and getting a more fulfilling job.

When we have a goal in mind, we can employ all our faculties to achieve it. What tends to happen is that other desires—compulsions--can seize us. It's that laziness that kicks in. It might not "look" lazy because we're actually doing something. But it puts important, more challenging work on the back burner while we "busy" ourselves with the unnecessary. We choose to escape the hard by distracting ourselves with the easy or arousing.

Therefore, we complain about being "busy" as a reason why we don't do certain things. Either those things are not important to us, or they are too daunting. "Busy" is our excuse for so much, and "busy" has become a virtue in itself. "Not having time" is a passive-aggressive way for us to dismiss the things we don't find to be important.

The Biblical story of Mary and Martha of Bethany is the focus of this chapter. Most of us see ourselves as Martha, who is taking care of the house while her sister Mary sat at Jesus' feet. Martha had become "distracted" by all the preparations, but she complained to Jesus that her sister wasn't helping. Although preparing the house is certainly important, and perhaps I need her to help me with mine, Martha lost sight of what was most important. She forgot that Jesus was there.

Like many of us, we become too consumed with satisfying our fickle desires or our need to be perfect on the outside. We forget what's "better," according to Jesus.

The story of Mary and Martha exemplifies the author's description of the active and contemplative life. He acknowledges that holy works are important, which is indicative of the active life. This is the life that is outwardly focused, even if noble intentions are at the heart of that life. Social justice activists will agree that this active life must have its roots in God, or else those efforts will falter as our self-seeking desires mask themselves as "nobility."

However, as our faith life deepens, we begin the inwardly-drawn practices. This looks like nothing on the outside. To the active, the contemplative doesn't look very busy, and this often frustrates the actives. That's why Martha complains to Jesus. She sees her sister resting at the feet of the Lord rather than helping Martha empty the dishwasher.

I'm sure if Mary—or even Jesus—asked Martha to sit for a moment to hear the Lord, she would say, "I don't have time." Mary probably knew that the dishwasher needed to be emptied, but she knew that Jesus wouldn't be at their house for too long. Her priority was Jesus, whereas Martha's was getting things prepared for Jesus so that he would be impressed. She knew the dishes would still be there when Jesus left, so she made the time to sit at his feet when he was with them.

How Mary chose to spend her time was different from Martha's. It might have looked like a waste on the outside, a moment of "leisure," but her energies were directed to someone greater than her ego.

Therefore, each moment of our day is an opportunity to devote time to God. From one moment to the next, where is our concern—growing in our relationship with God, or gaining approval from others?

CHAPTER 18

Active people still complain about contemplatives, just like Martha did about Mary. If a man or woman in any group in the world —religious or secular, I don't care—feels moved by grace to give up all outward business and live a contemplative life, their decision will be followed by their own brothers and sisters, all their closest friends, and many others. These people will make up many false and true stories about the deaths of men and women who gave them a good life, but they'll never make up a good story about those who stood strong.

I agree that many contemplatives have fallen away. They've become the devil's servants and contemplatives because they wouldn't follow true spiritual counsel. They've become hypocrites, heretics, or frenzied and slandered the Holy Church. I won't mention our concerns right now. If God allows it, people may be able to see what went wrong and why. We won't discuss them now.

◆ ◆ ◆

In the summer of 2020 during the height of the Black Lives Matter protests, a yoga activist account reposted a video from a black yoga teacher. She criticized all wellness advocates for "not doing enough" to support Black Lives Matter. She had disregard for posts such as "love is love," which tends to advocate for LGBTQ rights. In her mind, Black Lives Matter was the most important issue in the wellness community, and if we weren't openly advocating for the agenda of Black Lives Matter, then we shouldn't be in the wellness industry. Ok, I could go off on the many flaws in this argument, but it's inconsequential.

The Cloud recognizes criticism from the activists. Many times, activists will say that people aren't "doing enough" for their cause. Indeed, there are those who are most effective when they are doing something like protesting. Some are called to hunger strikes, others are called to march in Washington or petition their representatives in Congress. It's not to say that contemplatives don't perform these actions—many times out of their walk with God, they might use their talents or gifts to advocate for change in a particular arena. But for contemplatives, this isn't how they draw closer to God. Those who are active in their spiritual walk might not understand someone's call to solitude in the midst of so much unrest. But that's where they draw their energy. That's where they get grounded. That's where they tap into their center, which is why it's called in contemporary society "Centering Prayer."

This is where the lack of structure in a spiritual path can easily go astray. Without guidance, a contemplative can be led to hedonism or recluse. Structures keep guard over the sinful "thoughts" that can easily pull them off the path. They are like guardrails or trail markers, though resisting them can lead us into a pit or into the unmanageable brush. Without structure, we might even find ourselves back where we started. When we try to forge a new path without the structures of a religion—instead, resisting them—this is a lure of pride wanting to do things one's own way.

Some get so used to being physically alone that they actually reject society. Without community, it's easy to fall into pride. The Desert Mother Amma Syncletica once wrote that one can experience solitude in a community, but one doesn't necessarily experience solitude alone. She wrote:[23]

> *There are many who live in the mountains and behave as if they were in the town, and they are wasting their time. It is possible to be a solitary in one's mind while living in a crowd, and it is possible for one who is a solitary to live in*

the crowd of his own thoughts.

In other words, a contemplative life is not without troubles. The author of The Cloud mentions that there were many examples of contemplatives who have fallen into heresy. However, the contemplatives that remain strong aren't mentioned too often. They don't care to be heard or seen. Their desire is God, not fame or recognition. This humility allows them to keep them on the path.

CHAPTER 19

Some may think I don't respect Martha, the saint, because I compare her words about her sister to those of worldly men. I'm not disrespecting her or them. God forbid I criticize any of God's servants, especially His special saint, in this book. I think she should have been excused for her complaint given the time and place. She was simply naive. She probably hadn't heard of such perfection, so she didn't know what Mary was doing. She spoke kindly and briefly. She should be forgiven.

So, I think worldly men and women who live an active life should be excused for their complaining words, even if they're rude and show their lack of knowledge. Why? People today don't know what young disciples of God mean when they tell them to leave the world's business and become God's special servants in holiness and rightness of spirit. If they knew the truth, I bet they'd change their ways. Because they can't live anywhere else, I think they should be excused. When I think about the many mistakes I've made because I didn't know better, I think that if God were to forgive me for my ignorance, I would always excuse other people's mistakes. I don't treat others as I'd like to be treated.

❖ ❖ ❖

A woman in my prayer group criticized me for meditating. She told me, "That's not Catholic." She advised me to "do some research" on the criticisms of Fr. Thomas Keating and Centering Prayer. Indeed, I had seen one couple's "mission" against Centering Prayer and Keating—neither of them had any scholarly training in history, theology, or Scripture. It's easy to criticize what we don't understand. Perhaps we might speak from experience, such as the case of the woman in my prayer group. She got led down a dark path with her New Age and yoga practices, but I don't know if that dark path was a part of her that she glazed over through spiritual bypassing or if it emerged from teachers whose intentions are impure.

I remember a good friend from my Bible study group in Mississippi telling me that Donald Trump was a Christian. I pushed back on this, mostly because his words, actions and company do not reflect anything Christian. There doesn't even seem to be a fraction of imperfect humility. All I see is pride. But my friend maintained, "You don't know what's in his heart." Indeed, we do not. Instead, we speak from our own hearts and our own veils of perception. It's up to us to wipe clean our hearts and remove our veils.

Yoga and Buddhist teachings identify five common poisons of our mind. The first one, which spreads out into the others, is avidya or spiritual ignorance. This is the denial of a spiritual reality while mistaking our misperceptions and illusions to be reality. It is here we identify with the material—even our practices—without concern for the spiritual. It is emphasizing the outward-facing reality rather than seeing what might be going on inside the heart of another.

The author of The Cloud somewhat apologizes for his criticism of Martha in the previous chapter. Although he admits that those who are active in the spiritual life should see her as a role model, he admits that she, too, was loved by Jesus. Instead, when actives don't understand contemplatives, we shouldn't try to change their minds. Not everyone is called to the contemplative life, so we shouldn't exacerbate the division. Instead, we can recognize that the lack of understanding of the actives in regards to contemplatives is rooted in ignorance—or lack of spiritual understanding. If it's something they don't feel for themselves, they don't understand how others can be moved by God through doing very little on the outside. "They have experienced only one way of living—their own—and can imagine no other."[24] This lack of understanding is often what draws people away from religious life—they are turned off by the actives who want to believe their way is the only way.

CHAPTER 20

Contemplatives should keep themselves so busy in their heads that they don't care what others do or say about them. Mary did the same thing when Martha grumbled to Jesus. If we do the same as Mary, Jesus will bless us.

Martha implored Our Lord Jesus Christ to have Mary assist her in serving Him. Mary was more concerned about Jesus' love, so He replied for her. He was Mary's advocate, not merely defender. He called Martha's name twice to get her attention. He said, "You're busy and worried." Active people will always be busy doing many things. As charity asks, they should do these things first for themselves and subsequently for other Christians. Martha was doing excellent for her soul, so Jesus told her so. He said, "But one thing is necessary" so she wouldn't think it was the best thing to do.

What is best? Loving God is the most important thing. Martha couldn't love and praise God above all else while juggling life's demands. He said Mary had chosen the best part, which was hers forever. If you think about it, the beautiful love that starts here will last forever in paradise.

◆ ◆ ◆

The complaints of actives against the contemplatives had clearly been a problem since the author continues to press upon the defense of the contemplatives. The author continues to use the example of Mary[25] and Martha of Bethany to further emphasize how Jesus came to Mary's defense when Martha complained of Mary's lack of help. The author of The Cloud suggests that because Jesus knows what's in all of our hearts, he knew "Mary was deep in loving contemplation of his divinity and so he himself took her part."[26] He adds that Mary did not want to leave the presence of Jesus to defend herself. As the Acevedo Butcher translation suggests, many of us are too busy with everyday affairs, similar to what Jesus tells Martha. The author reminds us that what Martha was doing is important, particularly when it comes to attending to the needs of fellow Christians. However, this is not the only way.

We see this very evident in the criticism of contemplative practices. Indeed, there is some merit to this criticism because it reveals the self-centeredness of some New Age practices. An encyclical from the Vatican[27] conflates some of these New Age practices with Christian contemplation. Although the text doesn't say that Christian contemplation is wrong, it fails to understand the underpinnings of The Cloud. Although it's important to clarify for many Christians who want to pursue Eastern practices for psychological or physical well-being (and it says that it's perfectly acceptable), it reveals a similar problem that the author might have encountered in the 15th Century. Heresies and factions abound throughout Christian history (and continue to), but the author points out the words of Jesus, "But one thing is necessary. Mary has chosen the best part, which shall not be taken away from her."[28]

Therefore, those contemplatives who choose to love Jesus should continue to do so and ignore the criticism of those who don't understand. It's not worth the effort, and our pride might interfere in attempting to justify our position. This takes us further away from our singleness of purpose—the desire for God.

Similarly, I also wonder if the Marthas of the world—those who only want to prove others "wrong" about how they practice their faith in God--might be missing God in the process. Could perhaps their pride be getting in the way of their faith? If we are all professing a belief and devotion to God, why should we spend time telling others that the methods they employ are not the best ones? "If God is for us, who can be against us?"[29]

I'm also reminded of the story described in Acts 5 when the apostles were brought before the Sanhedrin. Gamaliel, one of the Pharisees, said some pretty profound words that the Marthas of the world might need to hear: "So in the present case I advise you: Leave these men alone. Let them go! For if their purpose or endeavor is of human origin, it will fail. But if it is from God, you will not be able to stop them. You may even find yourselves fighting against God."[30]

Indeed, we see Martha arguing with God himself, and He chooses to advocate for Mary.

CHAPTER 21

So Mary picked the "best." Wherever we say "best," we know that there is something "good" and "better" before it. Which "best" thing did Mary pick? The Church only recognizes two: active and contemplative. Martha is active and Mary is contemplative in this gospel story. No one is safe without these two lives, and no one can pick the best.

Our lives have three parts, and each is better than the other. Which three are placed uniquely in this writing? First, do good, honest acts of mercy and charity with your body. This is active living's first level. The second part of these two lives contains spiritual thoughts about suffering, Christ's death, and heaven. This is the second degree of active life and the first degree of contemplative life. Martha and Mary represent the contemplative and active lives in this passage. An active person can only reach full contemplation with special grace.

The third part of these two lives hangs in this dark cloud of unknowing, with God pressing many of their private loves to him. First and second parts are good, but third is best. Here's Mary's "best." Note that Jesus didn't say, "Mary chose the best life," because there are only two lives. He said, "Mary has chosen the best part, which won't be taken away." Both good and holy parts end with this life. We won't need to do good deeds or cry about how bad we are or what Christ went through in the next life. No one will starve or thirst, die from the cold, be sick, homeless, or in jail. No one will be buried because nobody will die. The third part Mary chose is for those who are chosen by God. Let him go for it with all his heart; it's his forever. Starting here will last forever.

Let our Lord's voice ring out on these things as if He were saying,

"Martha, Martha!" as He did to Mary and Martha. Hear Jesus saying, "Those living an active life should be as busy as possible in the first and second parts, and physically in both if they can. Don't disturb contemplatives. You don't see things their way, so let them live Mary's third and best part."

◆ ◆ ◆

The author continues to argue for the contemplatives, revisiting the words of Jesus, who said, "Mary has chosen the best part." Two words are worth elaborating on here—"best" and "part." The author understands that if we're given two choices, one can be "good" and another can be "better." But instead, Jesus uses the term "best,"[31] indicating a comparison of more than two. Rather than use the word "life," Jesus uses the term "part," indicating stages of life rather than an either/or dichotomy. It's also important to note that the author and Underhill were probably reading a translation such as Douay-Rheims, which says "best" rather than "better" or "good."

Returning to the previous chapters regarding the stages of life in the Church, there is an active life, involving important corporal works of mercy. This is considered the "lower" stage (or 'part') of Christian life. Although this stage is important—"good"—because it serves as the entry point of the Christian life, it is also outward-facing. We begin to turn inward at the "better" second stage/part, which continues some of these active works, but begins to contemplate deeper the spiritual truths, the Passion, and personal sinfulness. It is the higher active/lower contemplative stage, merging both "lives." Unless an active person is called by God to go deeper, this second stage is about as far as an active person goes. Similarly, a contemplative might return to this second stage if there is a great need for activism. The first and second stages can be lived while on earth, but both will be unnecessary in the afterlife.

However, the third and "best" part is the stage of the higher contemplative. As mentioned earlier, this third part can be lived while on earth, but in eternity, there is no need for corporal works of mercy or activism. An eternity without hunger or pain deems it unnecessary. The author writes,[32] "If God is calling you to the third part, lean on him and work hard, because it will never be taken away from you."

He also offers a more elaborate reply than Jesus to the actives who complain. He tells the actives to leave the contemplatives alone and at peace since this won't be taken away from them.

CHAPTER 22

The love between Jesus and Mary love was sweet. She cherished Him, and He loved her more. Whoever saw what happened between Him and her would see that she wanted to love Him so much that nothing below Him could comfort her or keep her heart from Him. This is the same Mary who couldn't be comforted by angels while crying at the tomb. When they told her, "Mary, no more crying! Our Lord is risen, and you will see Him live among His disciples in Galilee as He did." She sobbed for them because she thought anyone searching for the King of Angels would never stop.

In the gospel, there are many examples of her perfect love. They're written as if they were set up that way, but they were. If someone reads the gospel to learn about Jesus' special love for her, he'll learn that He wouldn't let anyone, not even her own sister, say anything bad about her unless He spoke up for her. He scolded Simon in his own home for whispering criticisms. Such great love.

◆ ◆ ◆

Aside from the Blessed Mother, there are a few women prominent in the New Testament. The first two, Mary and Martha of Bethany, are considered to be friends of Jesus and represent two important aspects of faith and works. Mary Magdalene, whom Jesus healed of seven demons, was also considered to be a friend of Jesus, particularly since she remained with Jesus at the tomb. A conflicted Samaritan woman meets Jesus at the well, and in the Gospel of Matthew, a Canaanite woman asks Jesus to heal her daughter. The Gospel of Luke describes a woman who was healed just by touching his garment. An unnamed woman was caught in adultery and was sentenced to be stoned, but Jesus intercedes. Although Mary of Bethany is noted in the Gospel of John as the one who anoints Jesus with perfume, she is unnamed in the Gospel of Matthew, Mark, and Luke when Jesus dines at Simon's house in Bethany.

Of these women in the gospels, the name "Mary" is weaved throughout. For centuries, Mary Magdalene was believed to be the woman caught in adultery or the "sinful woman" who anointed Jesus in Bethany. Because this "sinful woman" is also named Mary, the sister of Martha in Bethany, people often conflated the two. Mary Magdalene would also be branded a prostitute by Pope Gregory I.[33] We see this same error in The Cloud, where the author mixes Mary of Bethany with Mary Magdalene.

As a collective metaphor, this Mary is seen as a fellow sinner who looked to Jesus for healing and repentance. The first paragraph alludes to Mary Magdalene who stayed at the tomb after Jesus' crucifixion. We imagine her devotion as she sits by the tomb, confused at how this great man's life could end so tragically. At the time, she knew him as a teacher who could forgive sins. She would later see him resurrected and proclaim the Good News to the apostles.

The next paragraph doesn't specify Mary of Bethany until the end when he refers to Martha, her sister, and Simon the Leper's house. Even so, the author suggests that the collective story of "Mary" in the Gospels is an instruction of perfect love.

CHAPTER 23

If we fervently conform our love and our living, He will advocate for us by speaking secretly in the hearts of all those who say or think bad things about us. We won't be able to avoid them. If we don't care what they say or think and don't stop our spiritual work because of what they say and think, like Mary did, then I say our Lord will answer them in spirit, and they will be ashamed of what they say and think within a few days.

In the same way He answers for us in spirit, He will move other men in spirit to give us food and clothes if we don't leave His work for them. This proves they're wrong when they say men can't send women to serve God in a contemplative life without providing for their bodies. God helps those who help themselves, they say. They know this is wrong about God. If you truly turn away from the world and toward God, God will send you either abundance or the strength and patience to meet your needs. Whoever doubts this is either possessed by the devil or hasn't turned to God as he should. Never doubt this, no matter how strange or holy his reasons.

Choosing to be humbled by God's greatness and worthiness rather than your own misery will help you become a contemplative like Mary. Focus on God's worthiness, not your own misery. Nothing bad will happen to the truly humble. For why? They have God, who has plenty of everything, and whoever has Him doesn't need anything else in life.

◆ ◆ ◆

We continue to be assured that Jesus will respond to those who criticize the contemplative path. Rather than waste energy with this path, we should instead focus our energy on loving God alone. Those who criticize might have issues of their own that they choose to work out through you. You don't have to exacerbate those issues by giving them a logical response.

This chapter also speaks to the anxieties that often plague us in a distracted world. Oftentimes, we fear leaving the cares of the world behind because we feel God won't provide. God provides in one of two ways—by giving us what we need or allowing us to endure without. This trust is a true test of the contemplative path. If we doubt that God will provide, we might not be as committed to this path as what might appear. We might look contemplative to others, but inside, we are striving and clinging to the desires that pull us off the path.

Once the contemplative purges the attachments and aversions that keep us bound, we can focus on the "wonderful transcendence and goodness of God,"[34] which teaches us perfect humility. It is this perfect humility that ensures us of God's abundance and providence. As the London translation says, "[D]on't be distracted by the anxious concerns and complaints of your inner Martha."[35]

CHAPTER 24

Just as it is said of humility that it is truly and perfectly understood when it is beating on this dark cloud of unknowing, putting down and forgetting everything else, so it is also about the virtue of compassion.

Compassion means loving God above all else and loving others in God as ourselves. And that God is loved for himself seems right. This work consists only of a desire to please God for Himself.

Pure intention. A perfect apprentice in this work doesn't ask for pain relief, more food, or anything aside for God Himself. As long as His will is done, he doesn't care if he's in pain or happy. God is loved for who He is in this work. In this work, a perfect worker doesn't get distracted even by some of God's holiest creations.

This work seems to show compassion for fellow Christians. In this work, a perfect worker has no special regard for anyone, relative, friend, or foe. He considers all family, and he has no strangers. He has no enemies and no friends. So much so that he thinks people who hurt him and make him sick are his best and closest friends, and he wants the best for them as much as his closest friend.

◆ ◆ ◆

When we do something good for another, what is our intention? Is it to serve God, or is it to make us feel good about ourselves? Or is it to get on someone's good side so that they do something for us later?

An episode of "Friends" was concerned about this. Phoebe and Joey were debating whether or not a good deed could ever be selfless. Phoebe called Joey, telling him she let a bee sting her, saying that she didn't enjoy it, so it was selfless. Joey then told her that the bee probably died, so it wasn't considered a "good deed."

The author of The Cloud calls this a "naked intent." This is a pure intention to serve God alone without any expectation of favor from the other or desire to feel good as the result. Oftentimes when we do something, we expect at least a "Thank you," which tells us that we want to be appreciated for our good deeds.

When I worked in the television news industry, teenager Amber Coffman spent her Saturdays and Sundays feeding the homeless.[36] All day on Saturday she would enlist her friends and families to make sandwiches, and then Sunday morning she would go to City Hall to distribute them. She said Mother Teresa inspired her to help others.

One Sunday in December, my reporter and I covered her distributing "presents" to the poor. She had toys for the kids and toiletries for the adults. Most of the people we talked to were grateful, which I'm sure might have made Amber feel better.

What was interesting was that a homeless man approached my live truck asking for money. He had Amber's gift of toiletries in his hand as well as a bag of sandwiches. Sure, it wasn't enough to feed him for a week, but it was given to him freely.

"You just received gifts from a young girl, and now you're asking us for money," I asked.

He disregarded his gifts. "I don't need these," he said. "I need cash."

I was incensed at his lack of gratitude, which tells me that had I been the one who gave him the sandwich and toiletries, I would have been more pissed off. For me, if I do something good for someone I don't know, I expect at least a "thank you."

This suggests that my intentions for charitable actions aren't pure—or "naked" as The Cloud suggests. If our love for God is our pure intention, we would give freely to anyone—friend or foe—without the need for a thank you or a favor in return. If we intend to grow closer to God, then we hold no special favor for some people. We should consider all people—all creation—as brethren.

CHAPTER 25

I'm not saying you should have a particular bond with any man because of this work, whether a friend, foe, relative, or stranger. If this work is done flawlessly, everything under God will be forgotten, as it is for this work. By doing this task, you will become so kind and gentle that when you pray for a fellow Christian, your good intentions will be just as much for your opponent as for your friend or kin. Yes, sometimes more than your closest friend.

You don't have time to consider who is friend or foe, family or stranger. I'm not suggesting you won't sometimes or often feel more at home with fewer people. Compassion demands it. Christ was first friendly with John, Mary, and Peter. When you undertake this work, everything will feel like home because you'll only feel God. This shows how to love others as much as God.

Those humans were lost in Adam, and all who work to be saved will be saved because of what Christ did on the cross. A soul ideally oriented to this job and joined to God in spirit makes all people as perfect in this work as itself. If one part of our body hurts, it makes all the others sick, and if one area is healthy, it makes all the others happy. All Holy Church roles are alike. If we have compassion, Christ is our head and we are his limbs. Whoever wants to be a perfect follower of our Lord should labor for the redemption of all his brothers and sisters in nature, as our Lord did for His body on the cross. Not just His friends, family, and lovers, but everyone, without favoring some. His Passion will save anybody who turns from sin and asks for pardon. It's true of all virtues, not just humility and kindness. This tiny touch of love may be all they need.

◆ ◆ ◆

Although I enjoy Joel Osteen's verve, I'm always a little critical when he uses the term, "favor." He ensures his followers that if they follow Christ, God will reward them with "favor." This indicates a preference for his followers as if they'll get whatever they pray for. It doesn't quite work that way. When we truly "follow" Christ, we follow the Way of the Cross, meaning humility and sacrifice. We do things not out of expectation for reward or payback, but because that's what Jesus did. When Jesus healed the sick and fed the poor, he didn't say, "Ok, now you owe me." He just wanted people to follow his example and do the same. Rather than "favor," it's more about paying it forward.

I've learned that God doesn't play favorites. Think about it in a family situation. Although I'm not a parent myself, I know what it means for a parent to love a child. There has never in my entire life that I doubted my father's love for me. Sure, he would scold me when I would do something bad. Yes, I feared his wrath because he did have a hot temper. But his love for me was so perfect. His disciplines were just. But as much as my father loved me, he also loved my brother. Sure, I got into trouble a lot more than my brother ever did, but I never believed he played favorites. When he was suffering from dementia, I jokingly said, "I'm your favorite, right?" Even then he didn't answer.

We ourselves can look at loving others in this way. It's difficult, particularly when people really piss us off. Yes, I know I can't even look at Donald Trump without wanting to spit at him. But I know God loves him just like he loves me, even though Trump continues on his path of deception and delusion. That's his choice, and those choices will eventually lead to his fall. God doesn't will it, but he does allow people to make choices that bring about consequences.

When we're drawn towards contemplation, our hearts are eventually molded to be like God's. Sure, we might have a preference for our family and friends when it comes to prayer, but in contemplation, we drop all preferences and focus solely on God. Contemplation, just like any prayer practice, changes us.

We are continually growing in love through this practice to the extent that when we engage with others, this love echoes in our thoughts, words, and actions. We still love dearly those who are closest to us—that isn't abandoned in our lives. However, the contemplative "work" is aimed only at God.

The author writes that this work of contemplation can help others draw closer to God. Because we are all part of the one body of Christ, we all rejoice or mourn as one. The way Christ sacrificed himself on the cross, we give ourselves to others for the wellbeing of the community. This isn't just to help our family and friends, but for all.

CHAPTER 26

So, work hard and fast for a while, and then take a break. Yes, contemplatives have to work hard in this way. That's a lot of effort unless God gives you the grace or if you've done it for a long time.

But I ask, in what? Not in the sincere stirring of love that is always done to your will, not by you, but by the Almighty God, who is always ready to do this work in every soul that wants it.

What is this effort? All of this labor comes from forgetting everything God has ever made. This is man's work with God's help. God alone can stir love. Keep working, and I promise He won't fail.

Let's see how you handle working quickly. See how He stands by you? Work hard for a while, and you'll feel better about the workload. When you don't have devotion, it's hard and narrow, but when you do, it's easy and clear. God sometimes works by Himself, so you'll have little or no trouble. But never and rarely, only when He asks. Then He can work in you.

He may send a beam of spiritual light to cut through your cloud of ignorance. He may also reveal some of His secrets. Then His love will warm your heart, which is more than I can, may, or will say. I wouldn't dare use my fleshly tongue for God's work. Or, I wouldn't if I could. I'll tell you about the work a person does when grace stirs him. It's safer.

◆ ◆ ◆

Buddhist monk Mathieu Ricard once said, "Meditation is simple, but it's not easy." So many times we complicate meditation by telling people that we have to do this and that before we meditate. When we overwhelm ourselves with various disciplines that tell us what we should or shouldn't be doing or thinking, then we make it overly complex. We then layer it with so much esoteric language that turns off so many people who might benefit from it. Instead, we just need to do one thing—drop the thoughts.

This is why meditation is not easy. These complicated practices are geared to help us drop these thoughts. They help us focus in an increasingly distracted world. In Buddhist meditation or yogic meditation, we might employ mindfulness techniques or focus on a single object to aid in letting go of thoughts. I myself am somewhat critical of some techniques that tell us to "label" our emotions so we can recognize them later. What tends to happen—at least with me—is that I spend so much time trying to figure out exactly what I'm feeling that I catch myself in an endless dialogue of defining emotion. That might be helpful for someone who's caught in rumination, but maybe not.

Sometimes it's best just to tell yourself, "Shhh." We then remember why we're there—to still the excess chatter. The aim of Christian meditation—or contemplation—is God. We remember the desire for God. The emotion is love. The thought is to drop.

In terms of preparation, it really is individual. The yoga tradition—and many spiritual traditions—will have a set of disciplines or rules to live by so that we don't get ourselves into more dramatic situations. We might not be able to avoid dramatic people, but we can do our part not to contribute to the drama. We begin to purify our intentions—this practice helps us —so when we do enter conflict with another, we don't let them activate our own samskaras. Eventually, the waves of thought grow calm as we venture into deeper water. We essentially move past the breakers.

This is why spending time in solitude is important. We reflectively look at our lives to see where we participate in the drama. We create an intention to refrain from the same behavior —the act of repentance. But first, we must acknowledge our part in these mistakes and conflicts.

This time in reflection gives rise to these transgressions. It is difficult to admit where we've been wrong, but we can't move toward the mountain until we get ourselves back on the right path. Once we choose this path, we ask God to help us remain there.

The author writes, "God is always eager to work in the heart of one who has done all he can to prepare for the way of grace."[37] It indeed can be a labor, but the author presses us to continue. The reward will come with our hard work. He writes,

"As time goes by, however, you will feel a joyful enthusiasm for it and it will seem light and easy indeed. Then you will feel little or no constraint, for God will sometimes work in your spirit all by himself."[38]

However, this experience might not be described in words. It's important to maintain our imperfect humility, and not do so to satisfy our pride.

CHAPTER 27

First, I'll tell you who, when, how, and what tools to use. I'll also suggest a solution. Who will do this? Who left the world with a true will and chose a contemplative life? Everyone, even sinners, should cultivate this grace and work.

There's a man on Instagram whose profile says, "Wanna be a contemplative." In other words, he sees contemplation—or the contemplative life—as a goal, rather than a state of living. Sure, The Cloud indicates that before the contemplative life must come the active life. Seeing that this man is very "active" on Instagram trying to promote contemplative practices—which is good, he doesn't accept the possibility that being in the active life has merits of its own. In his book, Contemplative Prayer, Thomas Merton cites several saints and fellow contemplatives who indicate that in a monastery, Marys and Marthas (and even Lazaruses) are equally important.

However, this is concerned with the overall life choice in the monastery. Although Merton himself belonged to the Abbey of Gethsemani in Kentucky and lived in a small hermitage on the grounds, other monks had active positions within the monastery in making cheese. This, too, is essential in a community.

◆ ◆ ◆

So when the author of The Cloud writes about who should take up contemplative "work" versus active "work," he indicates that it is those who let go of the concerns of the active life. Like Merton, they do "need" those in the active "work" to maintain the community. Even Merton didn't devote himself totally to contemplative work. His writing and his public speaking about social and political concerns would draw him back to the world. It's clear he didn't let go of these concerns. He would even travel to Asia in the last weeks of his life to bridge the gap between Eastern and Western spiritualities. The contemplative life led him to this realization.

What we can also consider is the difference between the contemplative life, work, and prayer. This same man on Instagram was debating with another on who is a contemplative and who is not. The second man quoted Merton, indicating that it's like this exclusive, secret club. Indeed, some of the chapters in The Cloud make it seem like this—that we might have the desire to "be" a contemplative (like the first man indicates), but it's only by God's grace that we're chosen to be in this club. This sense of exclusivity misses the point.

Chapter 27 in The Cloud is one of the shortest, but it indicates that the work of contemplation is first a decision on our part. Underhill, who employs almost a direct translation of the original, uses the phrase "who should work," This indicates that it's a path we choose once we've "forsaken the world."[39] In the next sentence, the Johnston translation indicates contemplative prayer rather than contemplative life. This points to a modern approach to living outside of the monastery.

In contemplative prayer, we "forsake the world" by leaving our concerns and the concerns of the world in the cloud of forgetting. Our sole aim is to sit with God. In the contemplative life, we do the same by "forsaking" the worldly desires that keep the world bound in its carnal nature.

For example, I recently came across an article in the New York Times that highlighted a female director of pornographic films. She indicated that not all porn films are alike and that we can look at sexuality as "myriad and joyful," and focused on women's pleasure. It assumes that all people should embrace their sexuality and value pleasure. Like any of the "thoughts" indicated by Evagrius, our sexual desires can easily lead us into a cycle of craving-gratification. Although the Church sees adultery and premarital sex as "sinful," we can't ignore the other spiritual traditions that see these behaviors at their root—a pattern of attachment that leads to suffering.

Although sexual temptations seem to be much more rampant and overt in modern media, we also see more subtle cues of other temptations. Watch a commercial for a restaurant, and it will tempt you to eat food that might not be what's best. Watch a movie that emphasizes violence, and it will set fire to your anger. Influencers on Instagram like to highlight their hedonistic lifestyle. It's all part of "the world."

By "forsaking the world," we don't get lured by these "guilty pleasures." We're aware of how the "passions," in the original use of the term, surrender our sense of control and drive us way off course.

CHAPTER 28

People shouldn't start this work until they've forgiven themselves for past sins.

Because in this work, a soul dries up all the sin roots and causes that will always live in it, even after confession. Whoever wants to work on this project must first be clean. After doing what's right, you should proceed boldly but gently. It might feel you've waited a long time. This is the work a soul must do even if it's never done anything bad. As long as a soul lives in this dangerous body, it will see and feel this cloud of unknowing between him and God. Because of original sin, some of God's creatures or works will always remind it of God. And this is God's wisdom: When man was in charge of all other creatures, he ignored God's will and felt all the creatures below him press proudly above him, between him and God.

◆ ◆ ◆

Two points resonated with me in this chapter: The need for confession and our loss of sovereignty.

The Catholic Church still holds confession as one of its major sacraments, and it's definitely fallen by the wayside. I myself don't use it as often as I should—if at all. It's really uncomfortable to tell your darkest moments to a priest, especially if he knows you. Many times I've confessed to priests who do not know me. Once the priest gives you an act of penance—such as reciting a psalm, reconciling with another, or saying a rosary, you do feel rather free. It really is a rather liberating feeling that can't be described—only experienced.

However, many people—even Catholics—don't feel the need

to confess their sins to a priest. They feel that they can simply confess them to God in their prayers. Ok, as long as you do feel sorry for those sins—or you're at least aware that you've done something that caused you or another person pain. That awareness of your transgression as well as your resolve to do better the next time is important in keeping you on the path.

Two things typically happen in today's society. One is that we feel so guilty about sins that have nothing to do with us. We take on the unresolved problems of another. Others inflict pain on us and we blame ourselves. This is usually the case with victims of trauma or abuse. This is where therapy is needed to release that "guilt" that isn't ours.

Some of this "guilt" comes from within. We abuse ourselves with words or even behaviors for things that perhaps we've done. This, too, points to unresolved pain from our past. When we overly "hate" ourselves for how we look or for making a simple mistake, it's unreasonable self-loathing based on unrealistic demands we place on ourselves. They might stem from a parent or a sibling, or even a "friend" who had issues of their own.

The second thing that happens in society is the other side of the first. It is those who feel no desire to confess at all. They don't believe that what they do is wrong, and they blame others when they are implicated in something that goes wrong. This need for self-awareness—how our thoughts and behavior can cause suffering—is critical in aligning ourselves with God.

Even the pope goes to confession, which shows an internal compass that's aware of how a one-degree shift in direction can steer a boat way off course. Yoga's yamas (restraints) and niyamas (ethical observances) as well as the Buddhist Eightfold Path recognize the importance of having a moral compass. If we take an offset compass into meditation, we can be led down a path that leads not to God, but to more confusion and suffering.

The Cloud reminds us of our sovereignty over the created things on the earth. When the snake enticed Eve to eat from the Tree of Knowledge, it gave created things sovereignty over us. This metaphor is so prevalent today. Consider the many distractions that plague you at any given moment. Consider what urges arise just by scrolling through your phone.

If I scroll through my Instagram feed, here are some of the "sins" that arise: envy for a family or experiences, rage for the current political environment, and greed for more yoga pants. Scrolling the New York Times frustrates me as well, eliciting feelings of sloth because I feel helpless in alleviating the thorny divisions in society. It also elicits unnecessary fear as it brings me out of this present moment. It makes you worry about the future that hasn't happened, or it keeps you apathetic as you feed on worthless knowledge about what are the best wireless earbuds to buy.

Your emails entice you as well. They promise to satisfy our blog cravings. They tell us that we "need" this apparel to protect us from the cold. They elicit our fear of missing out, saying that if we don't act now, we'll miss these great savings. Our emails even tell us what TV shows to binge-watch so that we don't waste time with something more valuable—our spiritual lives. Clearly, we replaced God with our media and consumption choices.

It's clear that just looking at our media environment shows us that we lack sovereignty over ourselves. We even have various self-help programs and workshops that promise liberation over our fears and doubts. We allow other things to control us and pull us away from our center.

We can recognize this pull first through meditation. We dissolve this enticement into the cloud of forgetting. We give them a little bit of pause, saying, "No, you can wait, I'm doing something more important now." Eventually, the pesky desire dissolves and we continue to gaze inward.

CHAPTER 29

Whoever wants to regain the purity he lost because of sin and to be free from suffering should work hard and bear the pain of it, whether he was a sinner or not.

Even those who haven't done much wrong have trouble at this work. Sinners have more trouble than others, and for good reason. Sinners who have been bad for a long time often finish this work before saints. This is our Lord's kind miracle, as He gives His grace in a way that amazes the world. I hope God and all His gifts will eventually be easy to see. Some people now considered small or worthless as common sinners, and maybe some horrible sinners, will sit with the saints in His eyes. Some people who seem holy and are worshipped as angels, and some who have never done anything wrong, will sit sad in hell.

No matter what someone does in life, no one should judge the person. We should only judge good or bad actions.

❖ ❖ ❖

One of my favorite students was heartbroken. He found out that his girlfriend cheated on him. He's an honest man, and for someone to violate his trust was so far out of his scope of understanding. She is a nice girl, and this seemed uncharacteristic of her. I was his advisor, so I tried to uplift him, promising him that he deserves someone who cherishes his trust. I told him that there was something inside of her that led her astray, and it wasn't his fault that she betrayed him. I took his side and told him all the things he wanted to hear.

About six months later, he took her back. He would

eventually marry her as well. I felt like a fool because I had judged her for her misgivings. Because he loved her, he forgave her. He could see beyond her transgressions and trust their love. He was walking more closely to God than I was in this regard. Of course, relationship betrayals still arouse the thorns inside me based on how I was betrayed. But not every relationship was like the one that I had, and the lessons that come with them are unique to us.

There's a fine line between forgiveness and being a doormat. That line is attachment. When we suffer from attachment, we allow others to take advantage of us. We allow other things to take control of us because we fear being without them. This attachment can have many heads. If we forgive the person and allow them to continue their pattern of transgression, we must step away from the behaviors that harm us, even if it means letting that person go for a time. For my student, he was able to break up with her rather than shrug his shoulders and say, "Hmm, just don't do it again." His separation from her was enough for her to see the consequences of her transgression, but also for him to see beyond the transgression to recognize that their love was worth staying together. Not all relationships end up like this.

On the other hand, when we hold back forgiveness, even if the person holds no remorse for the transgression, we remain imprisoned at that moment. Our development snags in that area. We might succeed in other areas—professional, athletic, social—but we're limited because this lack of forgiveness snags our ability to move freely and move forward. It slows us down, and not in a good way.

However, God forgives. When we ask God for forgiveness, we ask him to set us free from the patterns that drove us toward our transgressions. Our contrite hearts aim for repentance. We want to get back on the right road and make adjustments to our lives to do so. This readjustment is difficult, like when a doctor resets a broken bone. We might have learned to walk one way, but eventually, we have to endure the pain of walking straight.

This suffering is necessary and purifying, but it frees us from the destructive suffering that our attachments bring.

Sometimes what happens when we hold back forgiveness is that we see the transgressor take on a new life. They've chosen to follow God, and things move so much better for them since they repented. When we see them, our resentment burns us. We get jealous, wondering how life can be so grand for this transgressor while we remain stuck in that person's transgression. We don't know what God has done in their hearts because we haven't let go of the resentment from our own.

People will say that forgiveness isn't for the other—it's for yourself. It's so you can move on from the transgressions of others and continue on your spiritual path. If the other person chooses to follow, then fine. If they continue in their ways, remaining stuck in their patterns, you don't let them hold you back from your freedom.

CHAPTER 30

Who will judge others' actions?
It's either given openly by the law and rules of the Holy Church or secretly in the spirit when the Holy Spirit stirs it up in perfect love. Each person should avoid blaming and condemning others' mistakes unless the Holy Spirit moves him. Otherwise, he can easily be led astray with pride. Judge yourself, and leave others alone.

◆ ◆ ◆

I confess that I've been judgmental of others. I look at the actions of some people and wonder if they have any soul at all. But we really don't know the wounds other people carry deep in their hearts to make them behave the way they do. We never know, if given the same circumstances and the same conditioning, if we will act the same way.

Eddie Murphy and Dan Aykroyd starred in the movie, Trading Places. Murphy played a con artist and Aykroyd played a stuffy, rich man of privilege. Two rich brothers used them to settle a debate between them—is bad behavior a matter of circumstance or a part of one's nature? The men strip Aykroyd's character of his privilege and frame him for crimes. They also hire Murphy's character at their lucrative firm, awarding him immediate privilege. As both characters react to their changing circumstances, they begin to mold their behavior. The film emphasizes nurture over nature.

A more recent example is the show, Ted Lasso. One of the most despicable, arrogant players on the soccer team was a product of a cruel father's ridicule and disrespect. We learn that his narcissism was his protective shell, and he earns our sympathy.

Most of the time, we don't see under the hood. We move about the world seeing the nurturing or lack of nurturing of others. When others don't behave in the way that we expect, we interpret their behavior based on what we believe is "right." We also use our "rightness" to deem others to be "wrong." Are we so sure that we're "right?" Do we really know the entirety of this circumstance? Do we have all the facts before we make the judgment, or do we judge first and ignore those facts that don't align with that judgment?

This chapter in The Cloud continues to appeal that we don't judge others. Although there are spiritual leaders who carefully weigh the situation before they make a judgment, we have to be careful when we casually make judgments about others. Our behavior towards that person might not show compassion, and we never know how our behavior might drive others away from God. We might be seen as a hypocrite, especially if the person is indeed innocent and we are guilty.

CHAPTER 31

As soon as you've made amends, start this work. If your past behaviors or new thoughts or feelings of sin stand between you and God, you must crush them with a strong love. Try to forget them as if they never happened to you or anyone. Put them down as often and as soon as they rise. You can try to get rid of them using spiritual tools or mental strategies. You'll learn these strategies best from God.

◆ ◆ ◆

Two things stand out for me in Chapter 31—"work" and "strategy." First of all, the author refers to contemplation as "work." This doesn't sound much like what we believe to be "prayer." Instead, it suggests to me to be a process. The author suggests an order of things—first, you confess your sins to help put your guilt behind you, then you engage in contemplative work. It is the process of undoing or unknowing the illusions that come between us and God. Even if we might have a relatively clean conscience—and I mean relatively in regards to oneself—we'll still have those pesky citta vrttis that pull us away from our practice. These can come in the form of "new" ideas that urge you to get off your seat and attend to them. You might feel inclined to intercede in the affairs of others, believing it to be "divinely inspired" because it came to you during your contemplative work. Rather than allow these thoughts to pull you out of contemplation, we "step above them" and leave them in the cloud of forgetting.

The second thing that strikes me is "strategy." Like Thomas

Merton's book, Contemplative Prayer, this book doesn't offer us any method of how to "do" contemplative prayer. It outlines the process conceptually, but it gives little instruction on ways we can stomp our mental stirrings under our feet. Sure, it tells us to maybe use a single word to help remind us what we're doing and realign ourselves towards desiring God. But after that, it leaves us to perhaps investigate methods from other traditions to help. Rather than endorse any particular strategy from another tradition, the author tells us to rely on God to teach us how to dissolve the chatter. One particular "way" might work for one person, but it might not work for us. Even 600 years later, The Vatican would tell us the same thing: "We therefore should allow God to decide the way he wishes to have us participate in his love."[40]

CHAPTER 32

I'll share my thoughts on these strategies. If possible, try them. Pretend you didn't know these thoughts were separating you from God. Look over their shoulders for what you think is God. If you do that, your trouble should end soon. If this strategy is well-planned, it's nothing more than a desire to feel and see God here. Love's desire always succeeds.

Another approach: When you can't beat these thoughts, surrender like a coward. You should give up fighting them and give yourself to God in their hands. You'll feel finished. If you test this strategy, I think it will dissolve everything into water. If this strategy is well-thought-out, it's knowing and feeling yourself as you really are—a wretch and a filthy person who's worse than nothing. That's humility. This humility gets God to take revenge on your enemies, pick you up, and lovingly dry your spiritual eyes, just like a parent does for a child about to die from wild pigs or bears.

◆ ◆ ◆

As a meditation teacher, I've both learned and taught many ways to slow down the thoughts in the mind. Many of them work for a time and some work during certain moments of my life. Although the author of The Cloud doesn't endorse a specific method of dissolving thoughts, he does suggest two approaches. One is to look beyond the thoughts and focus on God alone.

It reminds me of a man I worked with in Florida. People knew him to be a great social player, always "working" a room to ensure he talked with the "right" people. Someone noticed that he was always scanning the room, looking out for more important people to talk to. Perhaps he might be paying attention to the person before him, but he kept an eye out for others. Although this might be considered rude interpersonal behavior, it's a good way to deal with the excess mental chatter.

Perhaps an image here might help. If we're out in nature, we might fix our gaze on the mountain way ahead. It's so majestic, and it fills you with awe. You keep your eyes on it, even if there is something around you that might try to capture your attention. There might be an empty food tray nearby that irritates you, inciting thoughts about how careless people can be with the environment. You know once you're done admiring the mountain, you can tend to the food tray. You also know that getting upset over careless people won't solve the problem right now. Right now is the time for you to see the mountain, and you can tend to the other things later. You are aware of these things around you, and you trust your senses to alert you if you're in danger, but you remain still with your focus "above" rather than below.

Another approach is to give it to God. Yes, that sounds easy to say, but hard to do. When you give up fighting the incessant thoughts, you don't give them power. Instead, you give it to God. This might point to the possibility that you assume too much control over your everyday life, and God wants you to surrender. You might tell yourself and God, "I give up," or you could use your body to gesture surrender. Sometimes I will fall on my back and put a pillow under my upper back to "expose the heart." Other times I will prostrate myself on the floor. These two positions signify a bodily prayer of giving up control to let God enter.

CHAPTER 33

I won't tell you any more strategies because I think you can teach me more if you try them. I'm not there yet, even though I should be. Please help me for both of us.

Keep working hard, and if you can't learn these skills soon, be patient. It's your purgatory, and when all your pain is over and God has given you what you need and you've learned to use it, you'll be cleansed not only of sin but also of its pain. I don't mean original sin, but past sins. No matter how busy you are, you'll always feel that pain. It won't hurt as much as your past sins, and you'll still have to struggle. Because of original sin, sin will always be tempting. You must cut them down with a double-edged sword of wisdom. This shows there's no real security or rest in this life.

Don't go back and don't worry about failing. If you have the grace to get rid of the pain of your past special deeds in the way described, or better, then original sin or new stirrings of sin won't bother you much.

◆ ◆ ◆

The author of The Cloud recognizes that each person might have certain methods or techniques that aid in warding off distractions. At first, these techniques might be valuable in helping you sit in prayer. Eventually, you will have to use them less and less.

A podcaster who indicated that he had practiced Centering Prayer for more than a decade had interviewed a writer known for her books about Centering Prayer. He told her about the strength of the "prayer word"—which helps the person recommit the practice. He asked her when he would be able to let go of the prayer word. I thought this was a strange question because that really isn't the goal. If you find that during a prayer practice you don't need the prayer word, it doesn't mean that you've arrived at a new stage in contemplative prayer. It just means that you don't have many distractions or issues in your life that press upon you during your prayer practice.

Over time, yes, you find that your life "off the cushion" begins to shift. I hesitate to use the word "change" because it's still you, but a more discerning "you." Rather than have that second glass of wine, you're fine with just one. Rather than trying to get in the last word in a conflict, you remain patient and allow time to uncover the truth. You find yourself shedding things that don't align with what God is doing in you. You also find yourself spending more time and energy on things that generate compassion and health.

Because you're making wiser choices, you're not drumming up as much conflict with others. You eventually become less concerned with what others think of you. The lures that kept you hooked seem to miss you.

However, it doesn't mean you're completely off the hook. Some of those deep-seated issues might resurface. Even though you might notice an internal shift, it doesn't mean that other people are in this same walk. They might try to pull you off course and have you question your path. As long as we live on the earth and engage with our "usual" communities, we're never really "free" from those lures.

This is not to say that we should abandon our community or family and live deep in the Himalayas where no one can disturb us. Although that might protect us from any "new" temptation, it doesn't mean we're necessarily free from them. Giving up candy by not having it in the house might help abolish the addiction, but the true test is when we walk into a candy store.

CHAPTER 34

If you ask me how to get there, I'll ask the All-Powerful, Kind God to teach you. Because it's good for you to know I can't tell you. Only God can do that, and only in the souls He chooses. No saint or angel would want it without God's help. I think our Lord will do this as often, if not more often, in seasoned sinners than in newcomers. He will do this because He is all-merciful, all-powerful, and works as, where, and when needed.

He doesn't give or work in those who don't care for His grace. No soul, sinner or good, can have grace without God. Grace isn't given for good works or withheld for evil deeds. Note that I don't say "withdrawn" but "withheld." Be cautious, because the closer we get to the truth, the more we should avoid making mistakes. If you don't understand right away, put it next to you until God teaches you.

Pride offends God and emboldens sinners. If you were truly humble, you'd think God gives you the gift of contemplation for free. Being near this work allows a soul to feel this gift. Our ability to experience contemplation is tied to this work and will never leave you. If a soul doesn't do this work, it's dead and can't want it. This isn't about worldly will or desire, but something begins to stir you deep inside you that makes you want. If you're confused, don't give up. Instead, keep working by doing more.

Let it take you where it will without your interference. If you mess with it, you'll ruin everything. Be the right tree. Be the right house, and the right farmer will live there. Be blind and cut off your knowledge because it will hurt you. It's enough to like how something makes you feel, even if you don't know what it is, and to think about God when you do. Only focus on God.

If so, trust that God can move your will and desires without your help. Don't worry, the devil won't get close. Even if he's not very clever, he can only change a man's mind from afar. Even a good angel can't move your will, but God alone can. These words suggest (but experience proves) that no means can be used to "achieve" contemplation. Good practices prepare you for contemplation, but none lead to it.

◆ ◆ ◆

Although we might desire to "become" a contemplative, it doesn't necessarily mean that contemplation will occur. We might be well aware of the methods to open ourselves (and others) to a contemplative approach, but it doesn't make any guarantees that we'll "arrive" at contemplation. The best we can do is prepare our hearts, bodies, and minds for God to do his work. God chooses whom to give the gift of contemplation. It can't be earned.

I'm reminded of the story of the Prodigal Son, who left the comfortable home of his family to "experience" the world. Meanwhile, his older brother stayed at home and performed his duties as a son. When the prodigal son squandered his inheritance, he came home, pleading for his father to take him back so he could labor in the fields with other workers. Instead, his father opened his arms and restored his place as a son. This made the elder son jealous because he never left.

We, too, might see ourselves as the elder son who never sins, who "does everything right," even in prayer. Yet we are jealous when someone who eschewed God for a while, living a life of hedonism, receives the gift of contemplation. Perhaps they might continue to sin, which angers us even more. That still is God's choice to give the other the gift.

It comes down to what's in our hearts. Do we feel we deserve contemplation as a "favor" (as Joel Osteen would say)? If so, our hearts aren't open to contemplation. Our pride is coming between us and God. We're assuming God's gift of contemplation can be earned through certain practices. On the other hand, if we are contrite, if we are aware of our misgivings and transgressions and make an attempt to set our lives straight, this imperfect humility is the appropriate preparation to receive. In other words, we don't take God's gifts for granted, and we continually empty our hands so that we can always remain open to God's grace.

Similarly, it doesn't mean that someone who is inflicted with pride, lust, or anger will receive the gift of contemplation. If our hearts are directed elsewhere—if we have an ulterior motive other than a pure desire for the ineffable and the unknowable—[41]then we don't have the capacity to receive God's grace. Our cup is full of ourselves. That's why our preparation for contemplative work is about continually emptying ourselves so that we have true poverty of spirit.[42] We continue to let go of the things that come between our relationship with God and push them into the cloud of forgetting.

It's not that the methods or techniques that are practiced in the contemplative approach are useless. Sure, they are useless in that they don't guarantee us the gift of contemplation. Instead, these practices serve as a means of emptying ourselves so that we truly have the capacity to receive the gift.

However, we can be confident that if we have a desire for God alone—without a personal benefit—that desire comes from God.

CHAPTER 35

A contemplative apprentice should perform certain tasks. You may call them "Reading," "Thinking," and "Praying" These three are described better in another book, therefore I won't. I can tell you that all three are so connected together that it's hard for novices and profiteers—but not flawless people—to think adequately without first reading or hearing. A man will parrot the clergy when they preach God's message. Reading and reflecting should precede prayer.

Look a little more closely. God's word is compared to a mirror. The soul's eyes are reason, and your face is conscience. Just like you can't notice a dirty spot on your face without a mirror or someone else's help, the same is true for your soul. Sin-blinded souls can't see their guilt without God's word.

When a man sees in a physical or spiritual mirror or learns from others where he's unclean, he runs to the well to wash himself. Depending on the situation, this well is the Holy Church and this water is a confession. If it's simply a blind root and a little sin, God is gracious and this confession water suits. Beginners and profiteers can't think or pray successfully without reading or hearing first.

◆ ◆ ◆

The practice of Lectio Divina isn't specifically described in this chapter, but the practice is implied. As a starting point for contemplative practice, the author emphasizes the importance of reading, reflecting, and praying. These three components are the first of four in Lectio Divina, with the fourth being contemplation. The author understands that some people might not know how to read, so instead, they can hear the word of God preached in church. He compares it to a mirror that reflects our spiritual state. Our spiritual eyes are our ability to reason, and we look in the mirror at our conscience. Through this mirror, we might notice a stain on our faces. If so, we wash our face to remove the blemish or stain. The water is prayer or confession.

If we don't read or hear the word of God, then there is no mirror. The author writes, "Without reading or hearing God's word, a man who is spiritually blind on account of habitual sin is simply unable to see the foul stain on his conscience."[43] Indeed, if we don't have the means to align ourselves on the road to freedom, we might easily find ourselves moving in completely the wrong direction. As a former advocate of New Age spirituality, I can see how this occurs. Some of the reading from modern New Age writing contradicts itself in many ways. I won't go into specifics here, but it often leaves people like me more confused rather than inspired to love God.

The author also indicates that we use a bit of reason when hearing or reading the word of God. It's not that we seek the absolute and only interpretation—or even the literal—but we see the reading in its context with other texts. In other words, taking one verse out of the Bible might be used as a sword to cut a relationship with another, but taken in the whole of the Bible, our reason might see that our interpretation is not infused with the Holy Spirit, but our ego. Our reason might drive us to read further, or it might simply reflect on a few words that seem to resonate with us.

In Lectio Divina, the reflecting isn't necessarily a use of pure reason. It's not a Bible study, although those who are just beginning to read the Bible might need to do so. In my teaching of Lectio Divina on Insight Timer, my audience will often ask afterward what certain words mean or who certain people are. If I mention adultery in the context of the Psalms, it's important to understand that David committed adultery and his heart ached in his transgression.

This is possibly why the author emphasizes that beginners

should at least start with the Bible. Without that to serve as a foundation, it's difficult to make any discernment—reason. Then our spiritual eyes aren't able to see the reflection at all.

Eventually, once we have a bit of understanding in regards to what we're hearing or reading, we engage in this meditatio, or reflection. As a beginner, we might use it as a means of opening up our hearts to new understanding. This reflection, as a beginner, might even mean writing down what arrives in your mind as you try to make sense of it. In Lectio Divina as a prayer practice, it mostly means to repeat a phrase or word that seemed to have resonated with you at that moment. That keeps your mind anchored in the words rather than allowing it to flutter off to that yoga pose you're trying to master or what you might have to do later that day.

In this context, prayer is a means of recognizing how this passage applies to your life at this moment. If it makes you aware of a thought, attitude, or behavior that is pulling you away from God, then you ask God to help steer you toward him. If it fills your heart with love and adoration, stay there. If you're continually reminded of what is plaguing you, such as a conflict with another, then ask God for a better understanding of yourself and that person. This prayer in Lectio Divina is called oratio because it's our chance to do the speaking.

What follows our personal prayer is contemplation. This is when we remain silent, infused with God's word, sealed in our prayers to get closer to him. You can see how this practice is important, especially for those beginners, in preparing our hearts and minds for contemplation. This could also give us some insight into why many people struggle with meditation practices altogether—their hearts and minds are still fixed on the outside world. Contemplation requires us to tune inward, and this takes an investment of time.

CHAPTER 36

Those who do this work might have a sudden reflection on their pride and bad feelings or how good God is. They haven't read or heard anything to prepare them, and they haven't seen God's work. God, not people, should teach sudden pride and blindness. You could have more elaborate ways or words to reflect on God or sin, but avoid investigating or elaborating on the words themselves. It's fine to study them apart from this work, but not during contemplation. Instead, the words serve as a lump to contain your craziness. However, someone looking at you might think you're calm in body and face, whether you were sitting, walking, lying down, leaning, standing, or kneeling.

◆ ◆ ◆

Some religious and spiritual practices might whip us into an ecstatic state. Even some saints have described mystical experiences that might appear like a dream or vision. That's not what the author describes to be contemplation. Even if our feeling about sin whips us into a mental frenzy, we remain calm and peaceful on the outside.

Part of our "thinking" process is reflecting. This might occur outside of contemplation. We might write down some of our thoughts or have a conversation in our heads. We analyze and make conclusions or resolutions based on what we believe we know.

Some writers have referred to meditation or contemplation as "pondering," specifically when it is written in Luke 2:19, "Mary pondered these words in her heart." Pondering is a way of expanding or elaborating on what we hear. We might do this in the second component of Lectio Divina, which is *meditatio*, when we're called to "chew" on the words that resonate with us. This, too, is thinking. We're using our prefrontal cortex to think our way to God.

In contemplation, we try to remove the chatter. There is a time for prayer, reflection, contrition, and adoration, but there is also a time for receiving and rest. We do our best to quiet our minds and enter deeply into our hearts—where God dwells.

If a sudden awareness of sin or God emerges that is "uncaused," that is, we weren't thinking of them before we began, or if it seems to come out of nowhere, then this insight may come from God. It's not something we demand or expect. It simply arrives without our personal effort.

If it does arrive, it's important not to analyze them while you're having them. Just receive them. So often we provide a running commentary of what occurs in our lives. Rather than being absorbed in the beauty of a sunset, we feel the need to compare it with other sunsets, take pictures of it, or just remark to others how beautiful it is. Or if we see something tragic, which often occurs for me when I see a dead animal on the road, we don't get angry at whoever was unconscious and hit it or become disgusted at the destruction of natural habitats for our greedy, capitalistic gain. No.

Instead, we just experience it for the rawness it is. No elaboration, no reflection, no analyzing, no pondering. Just steady absorption.

CHAPTER 37

When contemplatives work hard at grace and practice, their prayers might suddenly arise out of nowhere like their thoughts. I'm referring to their own prayers, not the Holy Church's public prayers. Because true workers don't value private prayer over public prayer. Contemplatives pray publicly according to rules set by holy fathers. Their special prayers rise to God more quickly, without planning or preparation.

If words arise, which is rare, they should be brief. Less is more. I prefer a one-syllable word over a two-syllable word. This is especially true for the spirit's work, which should always be in its highest and most powerful part. Examine how nature works to confirm this. A man or woman, afraid of a sudden fire or man's death, must cry or pray for help. How? No, not even in a two-syllable word. How come? He thinks long and hard before expressing his needs and spirit. He jumps up and yells "fire" or "out."

And just like the word "fire" stirs and pierces the ears of those who hear it, so does a one-syllable word spoken or thought, but also secretly meant in the depth of spirit, which is also its height, because with spirituality, height, depth, and width are all the same. It reaches God more than any long, thoughtless psalm. This short prayer pierces heaven, the Bible says.

◆ ◆ ◆

When I attended a non-denominational Christian church in my 20s, I always admired those people who could pray aloud. It was so eloquent. One woman always warmed me with her ability to craft the most beautiful exhortations. They sounded just like the Psalms of David. Then when it was my turn to speak, I sounded like an idiot. I couldn't form words. My heart was lifted to God, but I couldn't speak out loud. I still really can't. After I lead a group through Lectio Divina or even a breath practice, words pour out of my mouth that echo the many things that I've read over the years. Everything seems to come together much more easily then, but they really aren't "prayers." They're more like meditations or reflections.

Similarly, I don't get much spiritual stirring when I pray the rosary or Our Father. I know many people live by these prayers and love the comfort of repetition. The Benedictines chant the Psalms several times a day, which not only is a beautiful practice, but it's also an admirable discipline. To be honest, I'd love to live a life where I could pause several times a day to stop and pray with my community. However, I usually have a class or a meeting at that time.

The author of The Cloud recognizes the importance of liturgical or communal prayer in the Catholic Church. Coming together as a community and reciting the prayers as one voice has value. Indeed, when the guy with that Trump mask is reciting the Our Father two pews away, you at least have one thing in common, just for that moment. You're laying your politics aside to lift your voice in prayer.

Although many people who follow my teachings don't attend a church because it doesn't "fulfill" them, that's not the point of church. The communal prayers of The Church are for the body of Christ as a whole rather than any personal edification. Attending church complements, rather than supplements, private prayer. Father Kelly once told me, "You think church is all about entertaining YOU?" When he said that, I was immediately vindicated. Indeed, we tend to be rather self-centered when it comes to communal prayer. We easily forget who is at the center.

Sure, I, too, used to get "God-high" every Sunday at my non-denominational church and feel I could take on the world. But when the rubber hit the road and I was confronted with the stress of the news industry, I would easily break apart.

When panic hits and your mind goes into fight-or-flight mode, you don't say, "hold on, I need to say the Our Father." You don't whip yourself into an ecstatic state, throw your arms in the air, and begin to recite the Psalms by heart. You say, "Help." No more than that is needed. It's one word that pours out from your circumstance. Why do you need more words than that?

Anne Lamott wrote a book several years ago saying that three of the best prayers you can say are "help," "thanks," and "wow." It's not necessary to elaborate more. It's possible, just not necessary, particularly if you're at a loss for more words than that.

The author of The Cloud uses the example of a fire in explaining the necessity of a simple word as an exhortation. If we need help, we simply ask for help. We don't go into a long soliloquy about why we need help or why we deserve it.

Contemplatives do the same. Although they will faithfully attend Mass or the Divine Office, their personal prayers don't use many words. If one emerges, it has concentrated power because it emerges from the depths of silence. Distilled, it can be read as:

"Just one short word perks up the ears of the heavens more than a thousand empty phrases."[44]

CHAPTER 38

How can a one-syllable prayer pierce heaven? Because it's prayed with the height, depth, width, and length of a full heart. It comes from within because it's spirit-powered. All the spirit's wits are in one syllable. If it didn't feel so strongly, it wouldn't cry so much. It wants the same for others as for itself.

In this time, a soul has understood Saint Paul's lesson with all the saints—not completely, but in a way and in part, as this work says—which is the length, breadth, height, and depth of the eternal, all-loving, all-powerful, and all-wise God. God's duration is His length. His love is vast. He's tall and strong. His wisdom is deep. God will soon hear from a soul so close to being made in his image. Yes, even if a person's soul is full of sin and he is God's enemy, he can learn to cry a single syllable from the top, bottom, length, and width of his spirit, and God will always hear and help him because his cry is so loud.

For example, even if someone is your enemy and you hear him screaming "fire" or "out" in the middle of winter, you would help him out of compassion. Lord! Since God's grace can make a person so merciful that he has mercy and pity for his enemy, what mercy and pity will God have for a spiritual cry in the soul, made and worked in the height, depth, length, and breadth of his spirit, which has everything by nature that a person has by God's grace? And He'll be merciful. Something that comes naturally from the spirit is closer to being eternal than grace.

◆ ◆ ◆

The author continues his explanation of how the short prayer can pierce the heavens. He quotes Ephesians 3:18-19, explaining that those who undergo contemplative work understand God in this way. He writes, "The length of God is his everlasting nature, his breadth is his love, his height is his power, and his depth is his wisdom."[45] Because this understanding of God is truly transformative, our short prayers emerge from the breadth, depth, height, and length of our spirit. Our short, simple prayer pierces God's heart in the same way someone yelling "Fire" pierces ours to act. It is automatic because it speaks from the deep, genuine anguish of our spirit.

Through this contemplative work, we understand that too many words aren't necessary. God knows the circumstances in our lives. While my family continues to struggle with my father's dementia and proper care, I don't need to explain what's going on to God the way I might to an old friend. When you speak to God daily, sometimes moment-by-moment with each breath, God is aware of the various stirrings in your heart. Rather than spend so much time in prayer trying to argue your case like a long-winded lawyer, God knows you. Don't try to prove to God you're right. Maybe to a certain extent, you are. Nothing you tell him is news to him. So don't waste so many words trying to cut a deal with God, saying that if God does this, you'll do that.

Instead, allow the desire for God to pierce your heart. Dwell there for a while. Breathe. If a word emerges, say it. If tears come, let them. If you're moved to fall prostrate on the floor, do it. Continue to allow God to melt your heart. Open up and let him in.

CHAPTER 39

So, we should pray with our whole hearts not with many words. One word.

Which word? The one that fits the purpose of prayer. What's that? First, let's define prayer. Then we'll know which word.

Prayer is a sincere wish to receive good from God and avoid bad. Since all bad things are caused by or are sin, we shouldn't use other words when praying to remove the bad things. Say or think "sin" instead. If we want good things to happen, we should pray nothing but the word "God" because God is good by nature and by action. Don't be surprised I prioritized these words. If I could find shorter words that covered good and evil as well as these two do, I would have used them instead, and I suggest you do the same.

You can't find words by studying; you can only get them by God's grace. Although words aren't necessary for prayer, if God gives you a word, use it and don't let it go. Even though these one-word prayers are short, you can pray them as often as necessary. It's prayed for as long as the spirit lasts, so it never stops until it gets what it wants. Remember how people won't stop crying "out" or "fire" until they get the relief they need.

◆ ◆ ◆

In the Letter to the Bishops of the Catholic Church on Some Aspects of Christian Meditation,[46] prayer is defined to be a "personal, intimate and profound dialogue between man and God." This "dialogue" indicates an exchange of words between two people. These words might change according to the situations in our lives. One day our prayers might be directed toward a specific petition for help. On other days, our prayers might be for thanksgiving. The author of The Cloud defines prayer much more simply:

"In itself, prayer is nothing else than a devout setting of our will in the direction of God to get good and remove evil."[47] This definition of prayer precedes words themselves. After all, our will might be inclined towards power or pride, but we can dress up words to make them sound like a prayer. Jesus gives us a clear example of this in the Gospel of Luke with the parable of the Pharisee and the tax collector. The Pharisee's prayer gives thanks that he is unlike others such as the tax collector who sits in the back of the temple. He gives his argument that he is more devout because he fasts and tithes. On the surface, this might be a fine prayer.

In the Deep South, we joke that you can say anything you want about someone else as long as you end it with "bless their heart." Somehow, ending words of gossip or judgment about another sounds much better that way. "Her makeup was so smeared that she looked like a prostitute, bless her heart." In a sense, this is similar to the prayer of the Pharisee. We might believe we're "good" Christians, yet we still utter words of judgment, pride, or gossip. This allows us to puff ourselves up for a moment, but then we seal it with "bless her heart" so that we ensure to others that we're still Christians. Of course, we don't say these sorts of things in prayer—or do we? Do we assume that we know better than others about how to live, and by "praying for" them, we're only wanting them to live by our personal code? Similarly, do we want to change other people so we don't have to change?

Note that the author of The Cloud writes that prayer is less about what others do and more about realigning our will. Another translation says "prayer is simply a reverent, conscious openness to God,"[48] which suggests that we remain open-minded about where God wants us—not others—to go.

On the other hand, we have the prayer of the tax collector, who can't even look up. He only asks for mercy. He knows that his choice of vocation has brought harm to others and shame to himself, so his gestures and intention are about setting him back on the right course. Beyond words, the setting of his heart is the prayer itself. Therefore, the words we choose must be simple.

Although the Centering Prayer movement will have us choose a "sacred word" as a means of consent, this doesn't constitute the prayer itself. The "sacred word" realigns our will towards God and serves as a mantra. Other religious and spiritual traditions use similar words to keep their minds centered and anchored. This word serves a purpose.

However, the author of The Cloud indicates that this word is a prayer in itself. Rather than "Maranatha" (a word I've chosen before) or "peace," the author of The Cloud suggests "God" or "sin." He tells us to use either of these words to signify what he believes to be prayer. We say "God" to ask God to "get good" or realign our thoughts and behaviors towards God. We say "sin" to ask God to help us "remove evil." He writes that he couldn't think of words any shorter than these, but if another word helps us lean towards what's good and refrain from what's bad, use it.

We might not even be inclined to use words at all. If our hearts are open towards God and our minds aren't so inclined to stray, then remain silent. This can be done at any time—while driving, washing dishes, or walking the dog. We don't need to only engage in this prayer practice by carving out formal times during the day. A simple word to remind us of our intention to serve God is enough.

CHAPTER 40

Try filling your spirit with the spiritual meaning of the word "sin," without paying special attention to any kind of sinful thoughts or actions, whether it's a small one or a big one, like pride, anger, envy, covetousness, laziness, gluttony, or lust. What does it mean to contemplatives, what sin it is, or how bad it is? For all their sins seem big to them, at least for this work, and even the smallest sin separates them from God and takes away their peace of mind.

Think of sin more as a lump, of what you don't know, but of yourself. If your spirit says, "sin," it's a desire to let sin go from your life. This spiritual cry is best taught from God than from a person. It's also best when done without particular thoughts or words. Sometimes the spirit overflows with words, flooding body and soul with misery and sin.

You should regard "God" similarly. Fill your spirit with the spiritual meaning of it, without paying special attention to God's works, whether they are good, better, or best of all, or to any virtue worked in a person's soul by any grace, whether it is humility or charity, patience or abstinence, hope, faith, or sobriety, chastity or willful poverty. And contemplatives? Because everything has its cause and existence in Him, they discover all virtues in God. Because they assume God will make everything good, they want nothing else but God. God is everything, so let nothing else work in your mind or will.

As long as you live this horrible existence, you'll always feel this filthy, stinking mass of sin as if it were part of your flesh. You'll use "sin" and "God" differently. If you had God, you wouldn't have sin, and vice versa.

◆ ◆ ◆

So often during my day a flash of my past will flood my consciousness. It's truly strange because nothing precipitated it. I'll remember something I said or did that was truly wretched, and it shocks me so much that I say, "Jesus is Lord" or "Lord, have mercy." It's something so automatic, like the need to say "bless you" when someone sneezes. If anything, it's a reminder throughout my day that I am not perfect and I have definitely not led a perfect life. I've made the most ridiculous choices based on my unruly desires, only to have me fall flat on my face. Every time.

This doesn't happen so much for me during my prayer time, particularly during contemplative practice. However, I know some people who cannot handle the guilt or mistakes that might explode in their heads once they remain quiet. It plagues them again and again, and it often results in abandoning quiet, contemplative practices altogether. It's a shame because they might not be looking at things holistically—working on their psychological states through either therapy or deep, analytical reflection while also working on their spiritual states through quiet practices.

In other words, I don't advocate those who suffer from trauma adopt a meditation practice without sifting through this trauma with a licensed counselor (with an emphasis on LICENSED). It might be that body practices such as yoga asana can still the mind while moving the body. For myself, if I'm in a state of hot anger, the last thing I want to do is sit in a quiet practice. A good run or bike ride exhausts that excess surge of energy.

Some meditation teachers will suggest mindfulness to help loosen the grip of ruminative thoughts. This is helpful if you can get out of the emotional cycle by accessing the logical mind. When a repetitive, nagging thought comes into the mind and tells you that you MUST jump on that train of thought, you reengage your awareness of the present moment by saying, "I know that I'm engaging in repetitive thoughts" or "I am aware that I'm jumping on a train of thought." You then return to something in the present moment, such as your breath or a body sensation.

Other meditation teachers will employ a mantra to help keep you anchored in the present moment. When your mind drifts off, you speak the mantra (or sacred word) to put you back on the path. Even the Catholic rosary, using the motor skills of your fingers to move the beads while also repeating the Hail Mary and Our Father, serves as a guided meditation so your thoughts can't drift towards unruly thoughts.

The author of The Cloud continues his discourse on using "God" and "sin" as simple words during contemplative work. Whereas discursive prayer might elaborate on a particular sin, asking God for forgiveness or mercy, the author suggests keeping it simple. It could be tempting to reflect on a particular sin, such as anger, but this might involve too much thinking and analyzing. Instead, we're asked to consider the "lump" of sin overall, like a lump in the throat. We don't sit there and try to think about what kind of lump it is that's choking us, we simply want to get it out of us. So even before the word "sin" arrives in our consciousness, we use that lump as a short prayer to guide us away from sinful behavior in our lives.

Similarly, he also suggests "God" as the counterbalancing prayer word. Many evangelicals will say not to pray for patience because then God will put you further away from what you're anticipating. That always sounded mean to me. Patience is a fruit—an outcome—of the Holy Spirit rather than a "gift." However, you can pray for increased faith to help in enduring hardship. We might also want to meditate on spiritual virtues or gifts in hopes that they will serve as a spiritual infusion into our daily lives. Reading and reflecting on sacred works does that, too. Instead, the author suggests that "God" is a similar word to redirect us not to the many virtues, but to the entirety of God. He writes:

"Fill your spirit with its spiritual meaning, without concentrating particularly on any of his works, whether they be good, better, or best, physically or spiritually...All virtues they find and experience in God; for in him is everything, both by cause and by being."[49]

It all reverts to one thing—God alone. We remember the apophatic perspective that the author adopts—that our image of God is not God. Our reflecting upon the virtues might make us feel warm inside, and that might feel good and encourage us to do likewise. However, this might not suffice in interrupting the nagging thoughts of sin that might bubble during our contemplation. Before we analyze and reflect, we might say the word "sin" as a prayer for God to help us remove it. Above all, God alone is our pure intention.

CHAPTER 41

If you ask how much discretion you'll have in this work, I'll say, "None!" Use good judgment and moderation when you eat, drink, sleep, and protect your body from cold or heat. Practice temperance with your fellow Christian when you pray, read, or talk. You must use good judgment so that none of these things are excessive. I want you to keep doing this work each day of your life.

I can't guarantee you'll always be fresh. Sickness, unplanned changes in your body and mind, and other things nature needs will slow you down and pull you down from the peak of this work. Your mind should always attend to contemplation in work or will. Avoid sickness as much as possible to avoid becoming weak. This work requires a relaxed mind and body, I'm telling you.

God loves you, so take care of your body and mind. If illness saps your strength, stay in God's grace. Then everything will be fine. God appreciates your patience when you're sick or going through hard times than when you're happy and healthy.

◆ ◆ ◆

One of the niyamas—observances—in the yoga tradition that's been somewhat watered down is brahmacharya. It's essentially translated to be "walking/moving with God." Conceptually, it means adopting practices that keep your focus on God. Some ascetic traditions will translate this as celibacy, which wouldn't quite make yoga very popular in the modern world. Therefore, they loosely translate it to be "moderation." Even so, we don't practice this completely, even in yoga. We see the excessive emphasis on yoga poses on Instagram, showing off poses and moves that take years to master. How is this move or pose helping you "walk with God"?

We also we extremes in what we eat or drink. We indulge during the holidays only to go to the other extreme—detox and dieting—afterward. We work or exercise to extremes. "Go beyond your limits" is a common mantra in U.S. society, but it's not observed in yoga. Sure, there is walking the razor's edge so you're always moving forward—with God, but moving too far beyond your limits is strengthening your ego.

The Cloud mentions moderation in Chapter 41. In all things, we're called to eat, drink, and exercise in moderation. The Johnston translation advises, "keep to the middle path," which is also a Buddhist observance. We're called to live a healthy life —body, mind, and spirit. This means having God in mind in all that we do. With everything, we ask—is this the healthiest option in walking with God and dissolving my ego?

However, with contemplation, we abandon moderation. We're free to soar to the extreme, as long as we are physically and mentally healthy. Our life can become a contemplative prayer, "praying without ceasing,"[50] as long as everything we do is about walking with God.

CHAPTER 42

How can you know when you eat, sleep, and do other things? "Get what you can," I'd say. Do this work without stopping or thinking, and you'll know when to start and stop other work. I can't believe someone who does this work day and night without thinking would make visible mistakes, unless he's always been making mistakes.

If I woke up and focused on my soul's spiritual work, I'd be less concerned about when I ate, drank, slept, talked, and did other things. It's better to pay less attention to them than to obsess over setting limits or standards for them. Think about sin and God with blind love in your heart. You want God, not sin. You're sinful and wanted by God. You need God's help.

◆ ◆ ◆

This chapter continues about moderation with "outward" activities but openly indulges in the work of contemplation. When we become fully dedicated to the practice of devotion to God, all other things find their place without attachment. They find proper balance in our lives. Because contemplation becomes your center, your True North, you don't become obsessive about your secular work or exercise regime. All serve to fulfill your spiritual health. The proof is in how you behave "off the cushion."

The spiritual path isn't compartmentalized like your professional life or your social life. Meditation, contemplation, and prayer aren't what you "do," but instead they spill into other areas of your life. They inform your decisions and serve as a roadmap for living. Many yoga practitioners often say, "I used to think yoga was about certain postures, but I had no idea how transformative it was." Indeed. If it's truly spiritual, it is transformative. It might not happen in an instant, but it will chip away at anything that tempts you off the path. You begin to make better choices.

"Do this thing without ceasing and without care every day, and you will know well enough, with real discretion, when to begin and when to stop in everything else."[51]

This doesn't mean we become perfect on a linear scale. It's not like someone who practices for 10 years will be that much wiser than someone who has only practiced for one. It's mostly a matter of how much a person is willing to give up on the "old ways." Some might take a little longer in chipping free the various attachments that keep them bound.

"I cannot believe that a soul who goes on with this work with complete abandon, day and night, will make mistakes in mundane matters. If he does, he is, I think, the type who will always get things wrong."[52]

Some are completely unaware that they are bound at all, even though they continue to practice. They haven't abandoned their old patterns because they deny they have them.

A friend had dated a man whom she believed to be a sex addict. I don't know if he was or not, but she told me how they would spend most of their time together having sex. Neither was working at the time. When she felt she needed a break from him, he didn't want to honor that. He continued calling and texting her the weekend she and I went on a trip. We both agreed his behavior was rather obsessive.

What surprised me was that he not only practiced Transcendental Meditation but was also a teacher of it. This is not to say that his meditation practice was bad, but it's clear there were some unresolved issues. He told my friend that his meditation allowed him to go off his depression medication, which is often common with people who combine meditation with therapy. However, his behavior "off the mat" was not indicative of someone who has reoriented his mind towards moderation and healthy choices. Perhaps his meditation practice helped him cope with depression, but he still experienced—and indulged—his craving. We would expect this from beginning meditators or those who are still learning the path, but certainly not from teachers.

This isn't an isolated example. Although the news media and those outside of the Catholic Church are open to pointing out its history of sexual abuse, it doesn't mean that this abuse doesn't occur in other organizations. The yoga tradition has its own history of lauding teachers who have sexually abused students. Bikram Choudhury obviously doesn't speak of this in his book, but he does mention his indulgence in cars—dozens of them. These revelations don't bode well for those struggling with cravings. It might validate the craving or suggest the hypocrisy of the teaching, rather than the individual teacher.

It's not as though an experienced meditator never experiences cravings. Over time, we adopt practices that help us temper them. We recognize them as "lumps" that interfere with our relationship with God, and we do our best to moderate our relationship with them. It sometimes means doing without them for a time until we can redirect this craving toward a desire for God.

CHAPTER 43

God can help, not your mind or will. Put your thoughts and feelings about what you should do under God and walk above this cloud of forgetting. In this work, you must forget not only other creatures' actions or your own, but also your own actions for God and all other creatures' actions. A perfect lover must love what he loves more than himself and forget his false self.

You will hate and be tired of everything that works in your mind and will, except God. If not, it wouldn't be between you and God. You don't like to think about your false self because you feel sin, a foul, stinky lump, between you and God. Your inauthentic self feels like it's part of your body. It will seem essential.

Destroy all thinking and feeling about others and your false self. You can do this because all other creatures' thoughts and feelings depend on your own thinking. For if you work hard, when you've forgotten all other creatures and their works—and even your own—you'll still be aware of your false self between you and God. Before you can feel confident that your work is done, you must destroy your false self.

◆ ◆ ◆

We see a clear departure from Buddhist or yoga philosophy in this chapter. Whereas many meditations or mindfulness practices will either teach us to accept thoughts that come or to inquire into their nature, The Cloud teaches us to "hate" them. There is also a vein of self-loathing here, which is common in much of the Catholic tradition, mostly stemming from the guilt of sin. Perhaps this is why many modern people turn away from

Catholicism! The Dalai Lama himself couldn't understand the Western idea of self-loathing. That concept doesn't exist in his culture, or at least, it's not espoused.

However, when you look a little more deeply into the "hatred" of thoughts, it refers back to Evagrius' seven "thoughts" that plague a monk in his cell. These thoughts are the seven deadly sins. Many of these thoughts are seeds that flower into thoughts, attitudes, and behaviors that turn us off a spiritual path. It's easy to see how self-love can turn into pride. It's one thing when a thought enters your mind. It's another when it truly occupies your mind for a significant moment. Thich Nhat Hanh understands that we all have these "seeds," but we don't need to water them with our awareness. We don't need to label them as good or bad. We just look elsewhere. According to The Cloud, this "elsewhere" is God.

The challenge here, which coincides with hatred of any thought that isn't God, is about forgetting the self. So much of today's culture is too heavily focused on identity, culture, and "finding" the self, but The Cloud charges for us to lose it. Spending too much time determining "who we are" takes away valuable time that could be spent in contemplation. We are easily tempted to bring our identities with us when we enter into meditation, where they get strengthened. This is where The Cloud reconnects with Buddhism, Toltec wisdom, and yoga—the need to rid ourselves of the attachments and identities of the false self.

In meditation and eventually contemplation, we might arrive at a place where thoughts significantly slow. We still might be aware of this "self"—a "naked knowing and feeling of your own being"—that[53] puts a barrier between you and God. Once that dissolves, you've achieved the "perfect."

CHAPTER 44

You're asking how to get rid of your false self. If you think destroying it would destroy all self-centered thoughts, you're right. This can't happen without God's grace and your willingness to accept it. This power is spiritual sorrow.

In your sorrow, be wise. In times of sorrow, don't overwork your body or spirit. Instead, sob quietly. Anyone who can experience profound sadness in this way can deepen his faith. All other problems pale in comparison. This sadness permeates him. When sorrow comes, it cleanses the soul of sin and sin-caused pain. It prepares the soul for joy, which removes self-centeredness.

Take note, though. Unless this sorrow is filled with holy desire, no one could bear it in this life. If a soul didn't get comfort from how it works, it couldn't handle its pain. For as often as he wants to think and feel of his God in purity of spirit, as it may be here, but can't —for he always finds his thinking and feeling occupied and filled with a foul, stinking lump of himself—so often, he almost goes crazy from sorrow. He sobs, fights, curses, and swears. He's carrying such a heavy load that he cares less about himself and more about pleasing God. He doesn't want to give up, because that would be like the devil and against God. But he wants to be, and he plans to thank God for the worthiness and gift of his being, even though he wants to be without his mind and feelings.

Every soul will feel sorrow and desire, in some form. God allows His spiritual disciples to learn these things according to His good will and their ability in body and soul, degree and disposition, before they are completely joined to God in perfect charity, as found here, if God allows.

◆ ◆ ◆

Mental illness these days is so common, it's no wonder if any people in the U.S. don't experience some degree of depression or anxiety. The Cloud returns to this feeling of "being," similar to a caged bird that longs to be set free. It feels great sorrow, much more profound than sorrow as a result of circumstances in life. Although the author doesn't expound on this too much here, some insight into this sorrow based on St. John of the Cross might be helpful.

Those in spiritual or secular traditions often speak about the "Dark Night of the Soul," referring to a dark moment of teaching in one's life. It might seem like circumstances are grim to the point that there doesn't seem to be any hope. Sometimes people refer to their clinical depression in this way. Others might say it's a period of back luck. It's much more profound than that. It's a time of spiritual aridity where you are being weaned off the sensory pleasures in your life. St. John of the Cross doesn't call this the "Dark Night of the Soul," instead, he refers to this as a "Night of the Sense." It's a clearing of the field after the harvest.

Yes, it does feel like a deep depression. You just don't know how to make yourself feel better. There is one distinct difference between the Dark Night and depression—you still long for God. The author writes that we never seek to end our lives. You don't long for God to do anything in particular, but you endure it. You have a certain experience of surrender knowing that God still holds you, but you're in a spiritual winter. He writes, "Though he continues longing to be free of its awareness [of this sorrow], he wants very much to go on in existence, and he gives God heartfelt thanks for this precious gift."[54]

The author of The Cloud tells us not to uproot anything. We often feel the need to "do something" to get us out of our sorrow. Indeed, it's important to discern whether it is depression or this spiritual sorrow. Rather than return to our old ways or seek new ascetic ones, the author tells us to "sit quite still, mute as if asleep, absorbed and sunk in sorrow."[55] St. John of the Cross gives us the same advice. Mind you, St. John of the Cross experienced the Dark Night while he was in an actual prison and couldn't escape.

This sorrow can be difficult to endure, but we are strengthened by our desire for God. We let go of the burden of the many attachments of our false self, our worldly self, and open our arms to God.

I think this summary from Daniel London's interpretation says it best:

> *Relinquish the part of you that believes you have earned your existence by virtue of your own personal greatness. Let go of the self who thinks that it holds value apart from its connection to God. Always remember that your existence is a gift, a gratuitous gift from the God who breathes you into being.[56]*

CHAPTER 45

Untrained and untested young disciples can be fooled by this work. If he isn't careful and doesn't listen to advice, he could lose his physical powers and fall into fantasy with his spiritual wits. Pride, lust, and cleverness cause all this.

So will this lie unfold. A young man or woman just starting the school of contemplation will hear this sorrow and desire: how a man should lift his heart to God and always want to feel his God's love. Out of curiosity, they think these words are fleshy and physical, not spiritual, and their hearts beat wildly. Because they lack grace, their pride and curiosity will push their veins and bodies so hard and rudely that, in a short time, they fall into frenzies, weariness, and an unsteady feebleness in body and soul, leading them to seek false and useless physical sensations. Or their asceticism can cause delirium or delusion. They may think it's the Holy Spirit's grace and goodness sparking a fire of love. This trickery causes hypocrisy, heresy, and error. False feelings lead to false knowing in the Devil's school, but true feelings lead to true knowing in God's school. Because, like God, Satan has contemplatives.

This trickery of false feeling and false knowing comes in many forms, depending on the states and subtle conditions of those who are tricked, just as the true feeling and knowing of the saved has many wonderful forms. I won't add any more of these lies besides the ones I think will be used against you if you do this work. Why should you know how to fool great clerks and powerful people? So I'll only tell you what might happen if you do this work. Be on your guard if it attacks you.

◆ ◆ ◆

I'm one of those people who needs exercise every day. There's something about getting my heart pumping hard or my muscles straining that gives me a mental release. I also feel better when new blood flushes through my system. In all honesty, a good run, a hard bike ride, or a heavy lift can really tame my emotions, particularly when my environment is particularly dampening my spirit.

As a yoga practitioner, I've also noticed a definite change in my emotional and physical energy after a solid practice. As a yoga and meditation instructor, I've seen the changes in my students. I remember feeling the energy significantly lighter in the room while cooling down from a hot yoga class. I thought, "Wow, this is interesting."

One of my most popular meditations on Insight Timer is called "Liberating the Heart Chakra." I hate that it's the first suggested track after my live sessions because I think it sends many of my students there after they've participated in a live meditation session. It continues to perpetuate its popularity because of its placement as a "suggested" track. I honestly wish I could change that and put a better, more authentic track there. I recorded it after I did it myself—I simply focused on words such as compassion and love for a few moments while focusing on the area in my mid-chest.

Although I won't go into how chakras are overused and misused in the West, there is a belief that if you focus on a particular body part, blood flows there. Leave it to the marketers to make a rhyme out of it so it's catchy: "Where attention goes, energy flows." I have experienced this physiologically myself. If I focus my attention on my hands during meditation, I feel a pulsing sensation there. Even yesterday during my treadmill run, I focused on my transverse abdominis muscles—making myself taller—so that I'm not compressing my lower back. No, there aren't chakras at the fingers or the TVA.

Two things are happening here. The tingling sensation of my fingers has to do more with meridians (Chinese acupuncture), nadis (yoga), or nerves. Being mindful of my TVA might not activate my TVA, but it helps me stand up straight.

The point is, these are physical sensations. Even the euphoria after a good run or the release after a hard yoga class is both physical sensations. Yes, they are tied to our mental states, because oftentimes our mental issues get manifested in our tissues. Our bodies are temples, but they aren't means of worship. We worship within them, so it's important to take care of them so they don't interfere with what's going on inside.

However, many practices conjure up this euphoria or buzzing sensation. Certain breath practices make me feel a little high. Some religious or spiritual traditions use psychedelics to move beyond their ordinary minds to experience the extraordinary. The brain conjures images and sensations that are different from the ordinary, and some will believe that this is where God can be found.

The Cloud says, "not so fast."

If unity with God was as easy as taking LSD, we'd all be tripping while still bringing on our drama and suffering. There would be no need for spiritual disciplines and observances. We'd never progress and learn how our perceptions and behavior cause suffering. The spiritual journey takes time, effort, and discernment. It doesn't come from a single acid trip. Those traditions that use psychedelics only do so during important rituals, and they are performed by those who possess the teachings and discernment of their long-held traditions.

The Cloud addresses how dangerous it can be when we assume that physical sensations are spiritual movements. Although these physical sensations might be pleasurable and ease our mental or physical stress, we have to be careful not to seek them for their own sake. We then associate pleasure with divine intervention, making decisions that have us chasing sensory pleasure over wise discernment. "Truly, from this deception and from its branches, many mischiefs come, much hypocrisy, and much error."[57]

Although The Cloud mentions that this can occur during

the novice stage of the spiritual path, we see examples of these teachings today. People will engage in spiritual theater, showing off these ecstasies in an attempt to build their spiritual following. Their followers might be wowed, stirring up feelings of envy to elicit the same within. We then create communities of esoteric, sensory practices that might be far from authentic.

"This is not true contemplative prayer. It's something bogus, the work of our spiritual enemy, the devil, and it is caused by feelings of self-importance, a love of being praised, undisciplined passions, and smug minds."[58]

Although I'm not a believer in numerology, how ironic that this is spelled out so explicitly in Chapter 45.

CHAPTER 46

Be careful with this work and don't overwork your heart. Instead of strength, use sincerity. Working through sincerity will make your experience humble and spiritual; working too aggressively makes it is bodily and beastly. Anyone with an egocentric heart who tries to touch this work's peak will be stoned. Hard, dry stones hurt when they hit you. Such impatient strainings are fleshy and graceless. They cause the soul to fester in demon fantasy. Beware of this animal-like disrespect and learn to love slowly, with a soft and demure body and soul. Obey our Lord's will quietly and politely; don't grab things like a hungry greyhound. I'll joke that you should stop the loud and big stirring of your spirit, just as you wouldn't let Him know how badly you want to see, have, or feel Him.

This may seem childish and silly. If a person had the grace to do and feel as I say, he should feel good playing with Him, like a child plays with a father.

◆ ◆ ◆

I used to teach an advanced yoga class on Friday nights. Few people would attend, and they could endure the more rigorous sequences required to melt the body into the "peak pose." Yet I still had beginners. Some came accidentally, but others would come with the intention of learning to handstand without the gradual training required.

Despite my softening the class to accommodate beginners, many of them would complain about wrist injuries. Their muscles and surrounding joints hadn't been adequately prepared. It also takes time to attain full body awareness in a physical inversion. Still, they would kick up several times in a handstand, forcing themselves even though they weren't ready.

In a physical yoga practice, you just can't skip the intermediate stages.

This chapter in The Cloud reflects the same idea. We can't force ourselves to experience union. Trying to bulldoze through long sessions in meditation before we're spiritually prepared doesn't earn that grace. We're trying to ascend the mountain before our lungs have acclimated, and it might hurt.

Instead, we walk and progress slowly with a sheer desire that's void of personal gain. Rather than vain efforts and extreme force, we "learn to love God with quiet, eager joy, at rest in body as in soul."[59]

CHAPTER 47

Don't be surprised by how I talk. I do it for a reason, and I've felt, thought, and said this to other God-loving friends and to you for a long time.

This is why I said to keep your true desires from God. For your benefit and to help you get what you want, I hope He will see it more clearly this way than any other way I can think of. I want to bring you out of the chaos of bodily feelings and into spiritual purity and depth. I want to help you tie a spiritual knot of burning love between you and God so you're both on the same page.

God is a spirit, so anyone who wants to be close to Him must be steady and deep in spirit, far from excessive outward expressions. God knows everything; no living thing or spirit can truly hide from Him. Because He is a spirit, things hidden in the spirit are known and shown to Him more clearly than outward expressions. By nature, a body is farther from God than a spirit. As long as our desire is mixed with any matter of the body, like when we stress and strain in spirit and body at the same time, it is farther from God than it should be. It would be better if it were done more seriously and slowly, in purity and with a deep spirit.

You can see why I'm telling you to act like a child and hide your desires from God. I didn't tell you to hide them completely because it's impossible. I said to keep it hidden because I want you to put them somewhere spiritual, away from any physical or emotional mixing that would make them less spiritual and further from God. Because I know that the more spiritual and less physical your desires, the closer you are to God, the more you please Him, and the more clearly you can see Him. You're more like Him when the spirit is pure, since He is a spirit.

This is also so God can't doesn't read your mind. You, I, and many others can imagine something physical that is said to be spiritual. If I told you to show God what was in your mind, you might have needed physical means to show something deep within you the way you might tell a friend. People will see something one way, but God sees it another.

◆ ◆ ◆

In his book, *The Presentation of Self in Everyday Life*, Erving Goffman theorizes that we become stage characters when we encounter others. We look to paint a particular impression before specific audiences to uphold a role in society.

In a profile about a YouTube influencer, the journalist noted that the influencer had a rather subdued personality until she knew the camera was turned on for the "real" interview. It was then the influencer adopted her bubbly YouTube persona. The question is, who was the "real" person? Was she playing a role on YouTube, or was that her "real" self, and her "character" was the one trying to make a good impression on the journalist? Or were neither characters her "real" self?

Spiritual traditions and social science disciplines both speak about the false self, which adopts various roles according to whom we encounter. But who are we when we are naked and alone with God? Is the way that we pray alone different from the way we pray with others?

The Cloud alludes to this surface self that feels the need to express emotions to be heard. The author suggests that we hide our desire for God, playing a little game of hide and seek with God. This might sound confusing at first, thinking that we can ever hide anything from God. But this game is mostly about securing our desire for God deep into our spirit so that we're not compelled to act out a "saintly" character in our prayer.

"You know well that God is a Spirit, and that anyone who desires to be united with Him must necessarily keep himself steadfastly in depth of spirit and far from all counterfeit things."[60]

On the surface level with our sensory distractions and emotional drama, our desire for God can get mired in this mix. However, the further we hide our desire for God deep into our spirit, the less it will be stained with the sensory or material world.

Gary Chapman (who doesn't have a degree in psychology) wrote a highly popular book on how we express love among others. These include spending time with someone, giving or receiving gifts, acts of service, or physical touch. Having this outward expression of love is more towards the active life rather than the contemplative life. Therefore, we love God more deeply than any "love language." With God, there's nothing to "show." There's no stage. For us to adopt a character to perform for God only makes this love tainted by worldly expectations.

CHAPTER 48

This isn't to discourage you from praying or speaking to God like you used to. I say this because I don't want you to stop saying "Good Jesus!" "Fair Jesus!" "Sweet Jesus!" No way! God forbid I leave what God has joined, body and spirit. As it should be, God will be served with both body and soul, and man will find happiness in both. As a sign of His promise, He will warm the spirits of His faithful servants in this life. As often as He wants, with sweetness and comforts galore. Some come from within, from an abundance of spiritual happiness and true devotion in the spirit. Such comfort and sweetness won't be taken for granted, and I hope others won't either.

Sounds, happiness, and sweetness that come from the outside suddenly should be avoided. They're good and bad. If they're good, an angel made them; if they're bad, a bad angel. This may not be a bad thing if their cleverness and uncontrolled fleshly desires are removed as I teach you or if you can do it better. How come? Because a pure spirit's sincere love stirs comfort. It was made by the all-powerful God without any help, so people should avoid fantasies and false ideas.

I don't think it's necessary to tell you how to judge other comforts, sounds, and sweet things right now. You may find it written by another man a thousand times better than I can, and you may find this better than it is. Why? I won't let you get what you want, and I won't let that stop me. You've shown me with words and now with deeds.

I can tell you about the good and bad sounds and smells that enter your mind. Use yourself constantly in this blind, devoted, misty love, and you won't hear about them. If you're still surprised by them because they're abrupt, it will tie your heart so tight that you won't give them much credit until the Holy Spirit of God or a wise father tells you to.

◆ ◆ ◆

I owe Grace Fellowship, a non-denominational Christian church in Timonium, Maryland, as one of the biggest catalysts in my faith journey. Never before did I meet such genuinely devoted lovers of God. From the moment you walk into its doors, you know that you're in a community of loving faith. They might not know you, but they welcome each person with open arms.

This church is also blessed with talented musicians and singers. You're truly moved when they sing beautiful songs of devotion and praise. You really feel the Holy Spirit swirling around and within you. It's truly remarkable and inexplicable.

One of the bands, a trio of sisters, played for my Wednesday Bible study group (which usually had between 100-150 women per week). When the lead singer was praying aloud, one of the sisters had her eyes closed and her head lifted high. Her palms were open to receive as she nodded her head.

Although I couldn't hear her, her lips repeatedly whispered, "Yes, Jesus. I love you, Jesus." What Jesus might have been saying to her, I don't know. But it was clear that her spiritual heart was profoundly stirred. Had she not been onstage, I think she would be doing the same thing. This wasn't part of the show. It was a genuine outpouring of what was going on within.

We can contrast that with some of the fire and brimstone performers on television and YouTube. I've seen the likes of people like Paula White, who performs before her congregation and claims to speak in tongues. It's not up to me to verify the authenticity of her trances, but I don't feel the same divine warmth with her as I did with the woman at Grace Fellowship.

The Cloud acknowledges that sometimes we might be moved to utterances as a response to what's going on within us. This sensory experience might offer us a glimpse of heaven, and we can react with awe. This stirring comes from within rather than a reaction from something we perceive on the outside. It's not as though being awestruck is a bad thing, such as being warmed by the beauty of a sunset or the playfulness of a puppy. Instead, we see if it stirs what's good within us. Does this increase our desire for God, compassion for others, or perceiving the truth, or does it keep us externally focused, looking to the outside world to kindle our faith? Does this inspire us to live undisciplined or extremely ascetically? If so, we should give pause.

Although the author of The Cloud doesn't give us a means of discernment in this chapter, he does tell us to remain steadfast in the work of contemplation until a spiritual director or God confirms our experience.

CHAPTER 49

Please follow this gentle stirring of love in your heart. It'll guide you in this life and the next. Without it, you can't live well or do good work. It's a good and right will to God, and a way to be happy and pleased with everything He does.

Perfection depends on goodwill. All sweetness and comfort, whether from a person or a spirit, are accidents and depend on good will. I call them "accidents" because having or not having them doesn't change the world. Not in heaven, though. In heaven, this sweetness and comfort will be unified with God and never leave, just as the body will be one with the soul. So on earth, they're just spiritual goodwill. I'm sure that if a person feels the perfection of this will as it can be had here, no sweetness or comfort in this life would make him as happy to not have it if that's what God wants as it would be to feel it and have it.

◆ ◆ ◆

In the First Book of Kings, God tells the prophet Elijah to go to the mountain and wait for God to pass by. After a great wind, an earthquake, and a fire erupted, a soft whisper remained. God can whip the wind, elicit an earthquake, and start a fire, but God is often in a still, small voice. We might be so amazed by the great works in creation, but can we attune to this soft whisper?

This goes back to the author's treatise on paying too much attention to the sensory. Sometimes we expect God to create wild miracles in our lives or within ourselves. We expect grand visions that descended upon many of the saints. We believe that the tingling sensations and highs are produced by God. Similar to wind, earthquake, and fire, God can create those, but so can mankind. These wonders are great and can stir our faith, but we can't place too much stock in them or only believe when they are present.

Instead, we must trust in the small voice, the meek stirring of love within us. This is where we must discipline our senses. If we continually play our music too loud, we cannot hear the subtle whispers. Similarly, if we're always looking to be entertained and aroused, we won't be sensitive enough to recognize where God might be quietly working.

This subtle love is present no matter what might happen in our lives. Sometimes calamity occurs, and all seems lost. We ask God why this happens, why us, and why God can't fix it. However, this soft stirring of love remains and trusts in whatever comes our way. It might not look good in the present moment, but we don't have all of the information God does.

A story from The Talmud illustrates this perfectly:

> [W]hen Rabbi Akiva was walking along the road and came to a certain city, he inquired about lodging and they did not give him any. He said: "Everything that God does, He does for the best." He went and slept in a field, and he had with him a rooster, a donkey, and a candle. A gust of wind came and extinguished the candle; a cat came and ate the rooster; and a lion came and ate the donkey. He said: "Everything that God does, He does for the best." That night, an army came and took the city into captivity. It turned out that Rabbi Akiva alone, who was not in the city and had no lit candle, noisy rooster or donkey to give away his location, was saved. He said to them: "Didn't I tell you? Everything that God does, He does for the best."[61]

CHAPTER 50

Our focus should be on this gentle stirring of love in our will. If it's polite and right to say so, we should be detached from all other sweetness and comforts, whether physical or spiritual. If they come, welcome them, but don't depend on them too much because they can weaken you. It takes strength to use up so much emotional energy for a long time. They might cause you to love God more when you have them, yet complaining when they're gone might show you love them more than God. If so, your love isn't pure or perfect. Pure and perfect love will feed and comfort the body despite sweet feelings and tears, but it won't complain. If God wants, your love can do without them. Some creatures rarely go without such comforts, while others rarely do.

All of this is God's will and plan for what different creatures need. Some creatures are so weak and sensitive in spirit that they can't handle life's temptations and trials from physical and spiritual enemies without sweet feelings. Some people are too weak to do penances. Our Lord's tears and sweet feelings will wash these creatures clean. Other people are so strong in spirit that they find enough comfort in their souls through reverent and gentle stirring of love and agreement of will that they don't need sweet comforts in their bodies. I don't know which is holier or more important to God.

◆ ◆ ◆

In the depths of winter 2019, I was struggling for answers. Each week when I would meet with my Ignatian prayer group, I kept saying the same thing, "Still no response, still unclear." I was incredibly depressed, doubting why I even moved to

Philadelphia when the pay and work were lousy and I was struggling to pay the bills.

Then, consolation came. During my prayer time, I wasn't thinking of anything, but an overwhelming sense of calm came over me. I felt steady and reassured, even though I didn't have an answer. To this day, I still don't have quite the answer, but I remember that sense of grounding. It holds me during moments of pain and suffering.

For many months I tried to recreate this overwhelm. I played the same music track, I sat in the same position, and I opened myself to the experience. I would get glimpses of it, but none was the same as that morning in January 2019.

The Cloud acknowledges that we might feel this consolation. For some, it might happen all the time. For others like me, it is seldom. What the author stresses is that we can't use these experiences as the sole indication of God's presence. In other words, if we're not experiencing this consolation, it doesn't mean God isn't holding us in the palm of His hand. It might even be that God is intending to strengthen us, weaning us off the consolation similar to being weaned off our mother's milk.[62]

We know that we're too attached to these consolations if we complain we're not having them. The author notes that some have the temperament to need more consolation than others. They might be weaker or more fragile spiritually. It doesn't necessarily mean that they are more favored by God. It might be that their worldly situation is direr, or that they have not been able to endure their struggles as others have.

These consolations are profoundly moving, but it's important not to rely on them or take them as the sole means of God's favor.

CHAPTER 51

Trust your heart's blind love. I mean in your spiritual heart, which is your will. Be careful not to confuse the physical and the spiritual. Curious and creative minds often make mistakes because they focus too much on their bodies.

I tell you to hide your desire from God. If I had told you to show God your desire, you might feel it more strongly in your body than if it's hidden. Because everything intentionally hidden is cast deep into the spirit. So, it's important to be careful when understanding spiritual words so you don't think of them as physical. "In" and "up" need special attention. Because spiritual seekers often get these two words wrong, which leads to mistakes and misunderstandings. What I know is based on proof and hearsay. From what I know, I'll explain these misunderstandings.

A young disciple on the spiritual path who has just turned away from the world says he has given himself to repentance and prayer for a short time and has been advised to go to confession so he can take on spiritual works he hears or reads about or even reads himself. When they read or hear about the spiritual path, especially "how a man will draw all his wit within himself" or "how he will climb above himself," they misunderstand these words because they are soul-blind and their natural wit is fleshly and interested in the esoteric. They believe they are called by grace because they have a natural desire for esoteric practices. If their counsel doesn't agree that they are called to this work, they argue with their counsel and think (and maybe tell others) that no one understands them. Because of the boldness and arrogance of their ego, they leave humble prayer and penance too soon and believe they have a full spiritual work inside them. It's neither physical nor spiritual work. Working against nature is the devil's main job. Because it's crazy and unwise, it's the easiest way to die physically and spiritually. Delusions can result because they think they're on the right path and focused on God.

◆ ◆ ◆

I fell onto the contemplative path by accident. I had been reading either Merton, Aquinas, or Augustine—I really don't remember—and I wondered what that meant. I was dutiful in the Church as a lector and a sponsor for RCIA. I learned *lectio divina* from a Benedictine nun and became curious about The Jesus Prayer, taught in *Way of a Pilgrim*. I bought and read a copy of *The Cloud of Unknowing* and found it rather confusing. Instead, I found Thomas Keating's work on Centering Prayer much more digestible. Although the practice of Centering Prayer in itself claims to be based on The Cloud, Keating, Menninger, and Pennington's psychological interpretation of contemplation is a diversion from *The Cloud*.

Some spiritual militants believe that Centering Prayer is contrary to contemplation, and it invites the devil into people's minds. I don't believe this to be the case. The practice of contemplation only grows what's already within you. If the devil hides there, then the devil will deceive the practitioner. I think it's rooted in what you hope to obtain from the practice. Are you drawn to contemplation because you want to be different and let your ego have its way? Or does the silence somehow beckon you, even though on the outside it looks like you're doing nothing?

I do believe that Centering Prayer can be a good practice for those who have the patience for a long, tough journey. I compare it to running. If you want to run a marathon, it takes hours of unrewarding long runs before you reach the finish line. If all you want to do is reach a finish line, run a 5K. Even if you reach several 5K finish lines, it won't get you closer to finishing a marathon. You have to prepare the body and mind over time to be able to run a marathon, and even still, there's no guarantee you'll get to the finish line.

In fact, marathon running is less about the finish and more about the lifestyle. You eventually make adjustments to your life —you eat better, you get more sleep, and you give up unhealthy habits just to be able to withstand the training. You don't need a runner's high or a finisher medal to be a marathon runner. You just prefer to run.

Centering Prayer isn't about wild imaginings or spiritual awakenings. It's not about the finish line of enlightenment. You just enjoy sitting in God's presence. You slow yourself down, open your heart, and become more aware of where God is. When your mind begins to wander towards what you have to do later that day or what mistakes you made in the past, you repeat your sacred word to redirect your mind to the prayer.

The practice of Centering Prayer doesn't involve some special call to grace the way that The Cloud suggests. That's what separates them. St.Teresa of Avila differentiates these two practices, even though she doesn't use the same terms that The Cloud or the Centering Prayer movement use. Centering Prayer might be a fine preparatory practice toward the contemplative path. Anyone can become a runner, just like anyone can practice Centering Prayer. What makes running and Centering Prayer sustainable over time is not diving in too deep at once and adjusting your life to make it more conducive.

Maybe you'll be called to do the work of contemplation that the anonymous author describes, but maybe not. I believe, though, that you'd be better suited for contemplative work if you practiced Centering Prayer than if you didn't pray at all. What's most important is to let God be the guide. Accept where you are rather than rush to get to a particular place.

The Cloud addresses those who try to hasten this work. What sometimes happens is the person is looking for enlightenment or sensory experience too quickly. They might confuse a sensory experience with a spiritual one and believe they are somehow chosen and favored by God to fast-track this work. This is where pride can easily manipulate and warp the work. In Wolters' interpretation, the author warns:

"Be careful not to interpret physically what is meant spiritually. The earthly and physical fancies of inventive imaginations are very fruitful of error."[63]

Sometimes if a person becomes too eager, a spiritual director might encourage the person to slow down. Using this running metaphor, it might be a coach or a doctor who sees a runner overtraining. They begin to see signs of injury, and they tell the runner to take time off. The runner's pride says, "I have a high threshold for pain" or "I have a body that heals quickly." The runner abandon's the advice of the coach or doctor and seeks community with those who are compulsively addicted to running. They find ways to keep running, to keep the runner's high, even though it is disastrous to the body. Then it's no longer running—it's an addiction to sensory pleasures.

In the Walsh interpretation, the author recognizes this same pattern with would-be contemplatives:

> *And so, without any hesitation, because of the arrogance and presumption which comes from his intellectual pride, he abandons humble prayer and penance far too early, and sets himself, or so he thinks, to true spiritual exercises within his soul. Such exercise, if it be rightly understood, is neither the work of the senses nor of the spirit. In a word, it is an unnatural activity and the devil is its architect. Here is the quickest way to death both of body and soul; for it is madness and not wisdom, and leads a man to madness.[64]*

CHAPTER 52

The madness begins when they read and hear that they should work from the inside out. They work wrong because they don't know the inside. Because they force their body's senses to turn inwards, which is against nature, as if they wanted to see, hear, smell, taste, and feel inwards. So they turn them around against nature and work their imaginations so hard that they turn their brains inside out. The devil can then give them false lights or sounds, sweet smells in their noses, wonderful tastes in their mouths, and strange heats and burnings in their breasts, bowels, backs, reins, and parts.

In this fantasy, they believe they have a peaceful vision of God that prevents useless thoughts. Because they're so full of lies, useless thoughts don't bother them. Because it's the same devil who gave them bad ideas when they were successful. The devil is careful in that in order to remain inconspicuous, he won't try to make them completely forget God.

◆ ◆ ◆

I've attended several yoga classes that employ the chakras, which are seven imaginary points up the spine and into the top of the skull. One of the most powerful yoga classes had us visualize these points while she struck a singing bowl that evidently resonates with each chakra. The meditation ended with one of the bowls "singing," which helped in the visualization of the chakras swirling in synchronicity. I got that tingling sensation you get, like a warm shower. Some say that's the kundalini rising, but I don't know. What I do know is that it was a nice way to recalibrate my focus away from the frustrations of my job.

Other yoga instructors don't do this very well. During one savasana, an instructor ended the practice by striking a singing bowl. She asked, "Did one chakra vibrate?" The other students, like me, sort of shrugged.

"That bowl is tuned for the heart chakra," she said. Ok, I thought, it's clear there's nothing inherent about the sound of that bowl that makes it resonate with the heart chakra. It is through the power of suggestion that it might.

I've also attended some classes where the instructors have you close your eyes and visualize the space between your eyebrows (the ajna, or the third eye chakra). Others will tell you to roll your eyes in the back of your head. That one kinda hurts, but I tried it.

One pseudoscience tradition—not taught in yoga classes—would have you focus on the pineal gland. According to them, it unlocks healing or awakening if you visualize it. I really don't think the brain works that way.

All of these visualization practices help in concentration because you aren't paying attention to outer distractions. The yoga tradition calls it pratyahara, which is the first step to tuning within. We begin to withdraw our senses from the outer world and learn to pay more attention to the inner workings of our consciousness.

In this chapter, the author notes how some beginners will seize these practices before they're ready. Their imaginations might run rampant, and they might see and hear things that verify their urgings from the ego. They might claim to hear insight from God, but it's their attachments running rampant in their minds.

It's not that using chakras as a means of training the mind is a bad thing. What sends us to madness or destructive choices is believing that's the path to God.

CHAPTER 53

Many wonderful things happen to those fooled by this false contemplation or any form of it, more than to God's true disciples, because they always do what is right. These others aren't. Whoever looks at them where they are sitting now, even with open eyes, would see them staring like lunatics and smirking like they saw the devil. The devil is close, so it's good they're careful. Some close their eyes and look like sheep ready to die. Some people tilt their heads like they have something in their ear. Hypocrites will use a mumbling chatter as if they're dead inside. Heretics and arrogant, pretentious errants cry and whine even when they're eager and quick to speak.

Many flaky and inauthentic practices look like this. Still, some continue in their practice out of curiosity while putting up a front before others. If only they can be seen behind the scenes. I think anyone who directly disagrees with them will see them explode at some point, even though they think everything they do is for God and the truth. Unless God performs a miracle soon, this "love for God" will make them go crazy and worship the devil. I'm not saying the devil has a perfect servant infected with all of these lies, but one or many may be. I say the devil doesn't have a perfect hypocrite or heretic on earth who isn't guilty of some of the things I have said or will talk about next, if God allows.

People with strange appearance habits tilt their heads to one side and lift their chins to hear. They gape like they should hear with their mouths. Some people point at their fingers, breasts, or the person they're talking to. Some can't sit, stand, or lie still without moving their feet or hands. Some people row with their arms while talking, as if they were swimming. Some people always smile and laugh, as if they were giggly girls and good-looking jugglers who couldn't act.

Authentic happiness and demure demeanor are preferable.

I'm not saying all of these bad habits are sins or that all of their practitioners are sinners. If these unseemly and unholy practices control the person who does them so much that he can't stop, then they are signs of pride and a desire to show off. They're signs of an unstable heart, a restless mind, and the book's unfinished business. I mentioned these so many lies. I mention these errancies so a contemplative can see how good his work could be.

◆ ◆ ◆

With exciting, arousing media available at their fingertips, my students become easily bored sitting in the classroom. Even when I'm teaching them a software program—a computer right there in front of them—they're still easily distracted by the text messages and notifications on their phones. Last week, one student couldn't understand how I got to a certain place in the software program because she had been busy pecking away at her phone.

This doesn't bode well for spiritual practices. Spiritual practices are slow and methodical. They require us to tune inward, which means turning off the outward noise. This is very difficult in a world that craves the next distraction after the first gets old after seven seconds.

You see what media goes viral. It's what's shocking and dramatic. It's an exaggerated reality. It's theater. People perform for their cameras—perhaps livestream it—in hopes of more likes, shares, and comments. They seek acclaim from the outer world, and even if they do, it's never enough.

How do you attract people to look inward? How can this be visualized on social media? It really can't. At best, you can describe it poorly in words, but even then, it's still incomplete. Perhaps you can show the effects of more quiet practices, such as a slow, peaceful countenance. It might attract some who are looking for just one moment of peace amongst the many videos of people performing stunts against a rap music soundtrack.

The Cloud vividly describes gestures and practices similar to modern-day Pentecostals or charismatics. On the outside, they appear to be in a trance. I've attended some charismatic healing masses where people collapse. Although I can't describe from my own experience what might be going on, neuroscientist Andrew Newberg has studied what happens physiologically. He noticed that certain parts of their brain are more active during these states, and the person is aware of their differentiation from others. They believe that God is talking to them and that God is an "other." Meanwhile, other parts of their brain become less active. Their verbal skills are inhibited, so words might sound like gibberish. Therefore, there is indeed something going on inside the minds of Pentecostals and charismatics.[65] Whether it is God speaking to them, I do not know.

What is interesting is that the author describes this movement in the late 14th Century, well before these movements would be revived in the 19th and 20th Centuries. Although he doesn't automatically discredit these practices or deem them to be sinful, he does advise us to give pause. As mentioned in previous chapters, we do not approach contemplative practices to feel good or for any sensory experience. We drop these desires and adopt only one—a desire for God.

The author also notes that these practices aren't part of contemplation. If we refer back to Newberg's work, we notice that Pentecostals feel a separation of self from God—an awareness of the individual. On the other hand, Buddhist meditators and Benedictine nuns have a completely different experience in the brain than Pentecostals. Whereas Pentecostals have an increase in the parietal lobe (which opens the awareness of self), Buddhist meditators and Benedictine nuns see a decrease in this area. Therefore, they become less aware of themselves and experience more of a sense of union. In this physiological sense, Buddhists and Benedictines are more aligned in this contemplative experience of union.

However, in a world that craves sensory experience,

contemplatives might not be attractive. They might seem boring. If we're looking for a wild trip, we might lean more toward the Pentecostals or charismatic movements. Some kundalini yoga practices might also give us a wild sensory ride. Regardless of what sensory practice we might choose, we remain careful about how easily we can become addicted to these sensory practices. They can easily lead us back to behaviors that keep us stuck.

Today's social media environment rewards pride, outlandishness, and exhibitionism. Therefore, it's not surprising that people are more drawn to parlor tricks than contemplative practices. Not to worry. Contemplative practices are magnetic, not dynamic. We keep a quiet, subdued demeanor as we move among the circus.

CHAPTER 54

Whoever does this work of contemplation rules body and spirit well, which gives them a healthy appearance. If the unluckiest person or people in this life could come here by God's grace, their luck would change so quickly and graciously that every good person who saw them would want to be with them and feel God's grace in their presence.

Anyone with God's grace should receive this gift because he can take care of himself and everything he wants. He can discern all natures and dispositions. He can be in the company of many types of people, sinners or not, without sinning himself. He can do this by being amazed by everything he sees and being an inspiration to others.

His words should be full of spiritual wisdom, fire, and fruit, and he should say them soberly, honestly, without lying or hypocritical piping. Some people are too concerned about seeing themselves from falling, using humble words and deeds of devotion. They care more about looking holy to others than being holy in God's eyes. These people will worry more and feel more sorrow over an unruly action or an unseemly or inappropriate word spoken in front of people than over a thousand useless thoughts and sinful stirrings within them or used carelessly in front of God, the saints, and the angels in heaven. Oh, Lord, pride leads to hypocritical speech. I agree that people who are truly humble should speak and act accordingly. I don't mean they'll have broken or loud voices against their natures. Why, if they're true, shouldn't their words be said firmly, clearly, and with spirit? And if someone who normally has a loud, clear voice says them in a low, squeaky voice—if he's sick in his body or if it's between him and God or his confessor—a that's clear sign of hypocrisy—

young or old.

How else can I describe these lies? Without the grace to stop being hypocritical, between their pride and meek words, the foolish soul may soon sink into sorrow.

◆ ◆ ◆

I think it was C.S. Lewis who said that we should behave in a good way, and our minds will follow. We also have heard the meme, "Fake it 'til you make it." Many people in the yoga tradition who faithfully attend physical yoga classes will say how it changes your behavior. Those who adopt a physical discipline such as running find their behavior outside of running change.

The Cloud has this flipped. He writes that if we engage in this contemplative work, we will change on the outside. It's hypocritical for us to try to act our way to a new method of thinking. He describes how others will speak differently while preaching and behave in another way when they think no one is looking.

It's a fine line, though. Contemplative work isn't just what happens while we're in prayer. It is a continual process of shedding and clearing any mess that accumulates over time. Here's an example.

My dog's water fountain—yes, I'm one of those dog owners—needs to be cleaned at least once a week. It appears to be giving clean water on the surface because the pan is clean. I know it needs cleaning because my dog begins to drink out of the other water bowl for my girl dog. He can smell that the water isn't clean.

If I run my fingers along the pan, which appears clean, I notice a bit of clear sludge. Then I pick up the pan and look deep within the fountain. I notice there are bits of something circulating in the water below. The easy solution would be for me to dump out the water from the reserve and clean the pan. However, if I take apart the whole fountain, I notice in the corners and inside the fittings, there is crud growing. I have to scrub all of the fittings and even the water pump itself so that the fountain can circulate clean water. It is only then that my dog will return to it.

The Cloud says that if we are genuine and pure in our contemplative work—if we're not self-seeking, people will naturally be attracted to us. There's no need to put on guiles to persuade people. Those who are ready to hear will hear you and will come. If there's anything impure, it will continue to grow within, and people will notice even if we don't.

Like the water fountain, God asks us to take a look underneath. We might empty ourselves and take in new water, but hidden in some of the crevices might be some degree of pride or envy that taint our message. We have to be vigilant in keeping ourselves clean so that God's message can be pure and attractive to others.

CHAPTER 55

So, Satan will fool some men. He will inspire them to keep God's law and rid others of sin. He won't tempt them with sensual and sinful pleasures. Instead, he makes them busy zealots who oversee Christian men's lives like an abbot watches his monks. These dogmatists remind others about their mistakes and their need to cleanse their souls, and they think this is their purpose. They say charity and God's love in their hearts motivate them. They're lying because hell is in their brains and minds.

The next part proves this. The devil is a spirit and has no body, just like an angel. If he or an angel requires a body with God's permission to help a person in this life, his body will be similar to the task he accomplishes. The Bible shows this. In the Old and New Testaments, whenever an angel was sent in the flesh, his purpose or message was evident, either by his name or by some instrument or quality of his body. The devil works in the same way. He displays what his servants are like in spirit when he appears in flesh. I've heard from people who can call on bad spirits and others to whom the devil has come in human form that the devil always has one huge, wide nostril, and he's eager to thrust it up so a person can gaze into it all the way to the top of his head. The devil only needs to have someone peer into his nostril to see hellfire, which can effect insanity. People who practice necromancy know this and can plan accordingly.

When the devil takes someone, he shows in some portion of his body what his servants are like spiritually. Because he fills his contemplatives' heads with hellfire, they blurt out weird ideas without thinking, then blame others for their blunders. This is because they only have one nose. Having two nostrils is a sign of good judgment in the afterlife. Even before he understands the complete effect of something said or done about him, he can tell good from terrible, bad from worse, and good from best. The brain understands a spiritual mind because it lives and operates in the head.

◆ ◆ ◆

Of all the chapters in The Cloud (so far), this is probably the most confusing. It literally talks about those who practice black magic and communicate with the dead. The author learns from them that the devil has one nostril. If people look up at this nostril, they will see the fire of hell and go insane. I was like, "Huh?" Carmen Acevedo Butcher's edition notes that the image of the devil with a single nostril was common in the medieval ages.

I was inclined to think about the yogic breathing practice of nadi shodhana, or alternate nostril breathing. The nadis are energy channels throughout the body. The yoga tradition teaches that the left nostril activates the ida nadi, and the right nostril activates the pingala nadi. The ida nadi is associated with imagination and creative thinking, whereas the pingala nadi activates the logical and rational. We need both to keep our minds in balance.

In this description of the single nostril, the author describes how the devil can use our imagination without the spirit of discernment or rational thought. If we only perceive with one nostril—our imagination, then it can run rampant within us. The author describes how church leaders, inflamed with the fire for God, can have a single nostril. Indeed, they have a passion for God, but it lacks reason. They therefore might be inclined to follow the letter of church law so strictly and criticize others for their transgressions.

We see this with many leaders in churches, spiritual groups, academic institutions, and government entities. In all of these groups, there are laws and routines that guide their members to stay true to the organization. What can happen is people become too attached to these laws, routines, and rituals to the point that they condemn too quickly those who advocate change. They get too fixed on the letter of the law and forget the spirit of it.[66] They set their lives on a specific mission, such as abortion or "family values,"[67] and fail to employ reason, compassion, or humility. What also occurs is that their spiritual pride gets so inflated on their mission that they fail to see—let alone correct—their own transgressions. Then they are seen as hypocrites because they don't practice what they preach.

When the author describes the devil as having a single nostril, it is a metaphor for spiritual discretion. While the imagination can be used as a creative means, the rational, discerning mind must determine where the devil and its lures can take root within us.

CHAPTER 56

Some people leave the common doctrine and the advice of the Holy Church out of pride, curiosity, and a desire to be clever. These people and their supporters overestimate their intelligence. They deserve a spiritual enemy-made fake sensation because they were never rooted in blind humility and living righteously. They exploded and cursed all the saints, sacraments, laws, and rules of the Holy Church. Men who live in the real world who think the Holy Church's rules are hard to change support these heretics quickly and easily. They think these people lead them along an easier way than the Holy Church.

Whoever doesn't want to work for heaven will take the easy way to hell. Each person should judge for himself, because I believe all such heretics and all those who support them, if they could be seen clearly as they will be on the last day, would be seen very soon entangled in the great and horrible sins of the world in their filthy flesh, secretly, without their arrogance in holding on to error, so they are rightly called Antichrist's followers. They're said to be nice in public but dirty sensation-seekers behind closed doors.

◆ ◆ ◆

"I'm spiritual, but not religious." This is the fastest-growing category in the United States. Most are bothered by the hypocrisy of many church leaders. Others are disgusted at the handling of sexual abuse. And still others in this category were burned by their religion early on, feeling that the tenets of their religious practice fall far away from the original teachings. I know many people in this category who were also turned off by their church's political leanings. These are people who should be heard because their voices can shape necessary change within some religious institutions. It's not that religious institutions need to continually modify according to the will of their people. Instead, certain practices that were necessary for years past due to a societal or structural need can be abandoned if it's no longer needed.

An example of this in the Catholic Church is the ringing of the bells at consecration. Before modern audio systems allow people in the back to hear what was going on at the altar, the church's congregation wouldn't know when the consecration occurred. Some people might have been outside, yet the ringing of the bell signaled to the people that the bread and wine were now consecrated.

Now that people can see and hear what's going on at the altar, the bells aren't necessary. However, the people of the church were outraged. They believed this was an integral part of the Mass and we were "losing" long-held traditions. They didn't want to change this for fear of other things changing. If the Church is a true living institution, it needs to continually question the essential practices, and update those that suited a temporal need.

In this chapter, the author somewhat addresses the "spiritual, but not religious" group. Indeed, there are those people who adopt their own spiritual disciplines to keep them grounded in spiritual virtues. These people do have a living, growing, fruitful faith that is continually nurtured by their prayers and rituals. However, the author notes that some are lukewarm because their pride or their intellect calls them to question the practices of their religious institution. Although this is understandable, rather than seek change within their institution, they abandon it altogether. They feel that the practices are too ascetic given modern life.

For example, sexual temptation seems to be prevalent in our society. It's difficult to go anywhere without seeing overt sexuality. Modern society validates "sexual freedom," but ignores the consequences such as STDs, pregnancy, and sexual exploitation. In its emphasis on "freedom," modern society trivializes it to be a merely sensual experience. It's no longer a profound union between individuals—although it can be. Instead, it's something to be done, only to go about the rest of the day. We might be satisfied for a moment, but the craving will remain.

In the demand for more freedom, we eschew religious practices that make us feel confined. We don't like a weekly commitment to a religious service, let alone a daily one. And we wonder why we don't feel connected to others.

Because we hate the rules and demands of our religious institutions, we flee from them. Without them, we have a less structured relationship with the transcendent. Without this structure, without discipline, we can easily backslide and let our sensory desires and our worldly concerns take over. They become our God. Our spiritual practices, perhaps strong just after we left the church, now get pushed to the back burner, after we finish our Crossfit workout, enjoy a good glass of wine, and settle into an evening with Netflix.

Our religious institutions not only keep us in a relationship with the transcendent, but they also remind us that suffering is natural. It doesn't make it easy, but it reminds us that we will encounter suffering. It not only teaches us to accept suffering but also provides us with healthy ways to endure it.

The world doesn't do that. The world teaches us that we can avoid suffering if we just engage in this sensory pleasure. It lures us into one pleasurable experience after another. When suffering is seen in the distance, we push it under the rug and buy something pretty from Lululemon.

Religious institutions, like therapy, teach us to have a healthy, humble relationship with ourselves. The practices are there to keep us grounded, not stifled. They center us. When we fall off our religious practices, our spirituality can become weakened. We then become vulnerable to charlatans who preach "favor" and "prosperity." We become addicted to this "feel good" practice that doesn't have any rules.

Yet when suffering comes, we are ill-equipped to handle it. And these practices do little to explain it. We then believe we've done something wrong to "deserve" it. We then lose our faith altogether.

CHAPTER 57

Let's talk about how young, arrogant disciples misunderstand the word "up."

If they read or hear someone else read or speak about lifting hearts to God, they'll know what to do as soon as they look at the stars as if they were above the moon and listen to an angel sing from heaven. These men will one day "pierce" the planets and the sky to look inside. These people will make a God that looks like them, dress Him in expensive clothes, and put Him on a throne that's never been seen on earth. These men make angels that look like people and play strange music with them.

The devil will fool some of these men. He will send a dew that angels think is food, as if it fell from the sky and landed sweetly in their mouths. They sit with their mouths open to catch flies. Even if it seems holy, it's all a lie because their hearts are empty. They're proud and tell lies because of how they work. So much so that the devil gives them false sounds, lights, and smells. They don't believe this because they think St. Martin saw God in a cloak with angels while working. St. Stephen, who saw Jesus in heaven, and other saints are also examples. They believe Christ's disciples saw him ascend to heaven as an example. So we should look up in reverence. I agree that we should raise our eyes and hands when praying. The work of our spirits shouldn't go up, down, left, right, forward, or backward like a physical thing. Our work be spiritual, not physical.

◆ ◆ ◆

When we're kids, we learn about "heaven above," and we believe that God in heaven is literally in the sky somewhere.

In the Creed, we say "He ascended into heaven," which further confuses us to believe God is "up there." The author writes that this isn't a physical "up" but a spiritual one.

I don't pretend to know the examples he describes, where people imagine God sitting on a celestial throne and angels take human form. I don't know if a particular group during his time promoted this view, but I do know some modern examples of this.

Some New Age disciples believe in the idea of "Starseeds," believing they were created from the dust of a faraway star. Evidently, some people can read a cosmic library and determine whether or not you're a Starseed or not. You can get certified to be one of these cosmic readers.

Starseeds are advanced spiritual beings, so of course, who wouldn't want to be one? They sound really cool, and most of them are trying to bring healing to all beings on this planet. They've even defined particular Starseeds according to what planet they're from. Jesus and the Blessed Mother apparently come from Sirius A.

I know what you're thinking because I'm thinking the same thing. Where do they get this stuff? From a physical, scientific perspective, this isn't possible. Even if you take it metaphorically, these adherents insist that it has some merit and validity in the physical world.

It's quite an imaginative explanation, and it gives something for the mind to elaborate on during meditation. If some people believe they are Starseeds from faraway planets endowed with the power to heal those on earth, I guess they aren't doing much harm. Perhaps they might inspire others to live a little more virtuously. Of course, I would imagine Starseeds would be against a COVID vaccination, which means that some might influence others to believe the same.

The Cloud mentions St. Martin and St. Stephen who saw visions during contemplation. Are these imaginings by Starseeds and cosmic readers the same as those from the saints? I don't know. But The Cloud says we don't look for God "up there" in Sirius A or Lyra. We can't send a space shuttle to these places, even if they are light-years away, so we can visit God.

Instead, when we say we look "up," it's a spiritual "up." It's recognizing our humility. It's a spiritual "looking up" that can't be explained, only felt deep within.

CHAPTER 58

People understood what happened with St. Martin and St. Stephen as miracles, even if they saw it with their eyes. St. Martin's cloak never touched Christ's body because He wasn't cold. Instead, it was a miracle to remind us we're all joined in Christ's spiritual body. Whoever clothes a poor person or does any other good deed for God's love to someone in need, in the flesh or in the spirit, does it to Christ's spirit and will be rewarded as if they had done it to Christ's body. Jesus says in the gospels that people often aren't satisfied until He performed a miracle. So He appeared to Saint Martin. All revelations have spiritual meanings. If the people could understand the spiritual meaning, the revelation wouldn't appear as a metaphor. Let's peel the bark and eat the kernel.

Not like these heretics, who act crazy because they drink from a beautiful cup then throw it away. We shouldn't do it, either. We shouldn't eat so much fruit we diminish the tree or drink so much we break the cup. The miracle, or the metaphor, is the tree and cup. The fruit and drink are metaphors similar to visible miracles and physical practices like raising our eyes and hands to heaven. If they are done to stir the spirit, then they are well done. If they are done out of hypocrisy, then they are not true. Why should they be looked down on if they are true and have spiritual fruit in them? Men will kiss the cup because it has wine in it.

Our Lord's mother and disciples saw Him ascend into the clouds when He went to heaven. Should we look up with our physical eyes to see if we can see Him in heaven, like St. Stephen? No, He didn't show Him to Saint Stephen in heaven in his body, because He wanted to show us that we should look up into heaven in our contemplative work to see Him as Saint Stephen did, either standing, sitting, or lying down. For no one cares if His body is standing, sitting, or lying in heaven. And it doesn't need to be said again that His body and soul are one and never leave each other.

It doesn't matter if He's sitting, standing, or lying down. It's important that He appears in these visions the way He wants to convey His message. If He shows Himself lying down, standing up, or sitting down in this life, it's for a spiritual reason, not because He has a body in heaven.

Example: Standing means you're willing to help. When a friend is in a physical battle, they say, "Bear well, friend, and fight fast." I'll help you fight, so don't give up. He doesn't just mean standing still. This battle could be on horseback instead of on foot, or it could be in motion instead of standing still. But he means that he will be ready to help him when he says he will stand by him. So, when St. Stephen was being killed for his faith, Jesus showed Himself to him in heaven. This wasn't to show us how to look up to heaven. As He told Saint Stephen in person about all those who are persecuted for loving Him, "Lo, Stephen! As surely as I open this physical sky, which is called 'heaven,' and let you see me standing there, you can be sure that I am standing next to you by the power of My Godhead. And I'm ready to help you, so stand firm in your faith and take the blows from those hard stones with courage. Everyone who suffers for Me will receive a crown of splendor. These physical displays were done to convey a spiritual meaning.

❖ ❖ ❖

If you've ever studied the Book of Revelation, or maybe even read a few lines of it, you'll see some pretty wild visions there. Whether these appeared as a vision of St. John's actual eyes or through dreams, we don't know. In the Old Testament, Joseph had been framed and imprisoned but had the ability to interpret dreams. He won favor of the king because he interpreted a recurring dream that would warn the king of future calamity.

Carl Jung believed that our dreams convey something happening in our lives. They might not make sense to us literally, but instead, they construct an interpretive message.

The author mentions St. Stephen and St. Martin, who both had visions of Christ. Although it's not clear whether these were visions of the physical eyes or spiritual eyes, the key is that we don't interpret them literally. Like Revelation, the visions or dreams that arrive in our lives don't communicate literal truth, such as Jesus holding seven stars and having a sword coming out of his mouth.[68]

Instead, we should look at them interpretively. The answer might not come quickly, but if our spiritual eyes are fixed on God, we might see the spiritual truth that is conveyed. It might not be something we're ready for just yet, but we continue on our spiritual path, aligning our actions and desires toward compassion and truth.

I'm still a little shocked by what I read yesterday about the New Age concepts. Some of the cosmic readers might actually have had visions or dreams about faraway planets and stars. They might have written them down, but their mistake is that they interpreted these visions and dreams literally. Much of what I read, such as the "lizard people" living in secret on the planet and infecting others with their desire for power, just seems crazy. It assumes that those people don't have a conscious choice to do good. It also assumes that the "light workers" will always choose good. If none of these people are aware of their "origin" on other planets and they don't recognize their "true" essence, don't they just live ordinary lives? Don't they do good and evil just like everyone else? What happens if someone from Lyra or Sirius A is born into poverty and suffers from parental abuse?

We can't always assume that spiritual dreams and visions only arrive for those who are living faithful lives. My guess is that God tries to communicate with all of us. At each moment, through each circumstance, God is speaking to us. Sometimes we might be so caught up in our suffering that we might see where God is working in other places. Or, in the case of disease, we might not see that through enduring our suffering, we might be a source of strength to those who might need it.

If the visions and dreams come to those who don't live faithful lives, perhaps they might have the insight to seek understanding. They won't say that the vision contains actual truth. Instead, they might see the spiritual meaning and begin the long journey of faith. On the other hand, they might build a whole empire around the literal message and believe that some people on earth are actually lizards or "Starseeds" from other planets.

God works in wondrous and mysterious ways. It's important for us to seek the spiritual truth beyond the vision.

CHAPTER 59

If you ask me about the ascension of our Lord, I'll tell you it happened in the flesh and had both a physical and spiritual meaning because He was both God and man. He was dead and dressed in immortality, just like us on Judgment Day. Our bodies and souls will be so subtle that we can move as quickly in them as in our minds. I hope everything is good then, as scribes say. Now, only spirits can go to heaven, not bodies. It will be so spiritual that it won't be like physically moving up, down, left, right, behind, or in front.

If they want to be contemplatives, especially in this book's work, they should be busy watching to make sure the stirring doesn't go up or down, in or out, or move from place to place. Even though it's called "rest," they won't think it's staying put. For the perfection of this work is so pure and spiritual in itself, it can be seen far away from any movement and any place.

It should be called a sudden change, not a place change. When working with spirits, forget time, place, and body. Be careful not to use Christ's bodily ascension as an example to stretch your imagination during prayer. Spiritually, this shouldn't be. You could use Christ's physical ascent to heaven as an example. God proves this by saying, "No man can go to heaven except He who came down from heaven and became a man for the love of man." If it were possible to physically ascend, which it probably isn't, it would only work through the power of the spirit rather than physical straining or stressing of our imaginations to go up, in, or to the side. You can believe in this lie, but it won't make it true.

❖ ❖ ❖

The author continues his discourse on the literal and metaphorical interpretation of "lift up," "go within," and "stirring." These aren't physical actions, such as an actual lifting up of our hearts or staring at our navel to "go within."

I remember on an old yoga tape the instructor said to "go within." At the time, I really didn't know what that meant. This term is often used in the yoga community. Even I say things like "turn inward." This isn't a physical action but an attentional one. Christian contemplatives call this "recollection," because we tune out the worldly desires and tune into the presence of God. It might not be felt physically, but it's felt spiritually.

Even the term "lift up" might incline us to puff up our chest —an actual "lifting up" of our sternum. This is good to expand our breathing and our posture, and it's a symbolic gesture of openness.

When we hear about internal stirring, this is difficult to explain. It's not a mental stirring, and it's not a physical one. However, both the mind and the body have to be still to notice the internal stirring.

A lot of New Age practitioners will confuse energy and spirit. I, too, have used them interchangeably. Energy is a physical entity. Like the wind, we can't see it, but we can notice when it's doing its work. Energy can be measured in the physical world. When I instruct my students to breathe in, they might feel more energized. They might also notice a calming energy after a breath session or meditation.

Energy isn't positive or negative. It can be used to light a home, or it can be used to ignite a bomb. It's the channel— the medium through which energy flows—that can be positive or negative. Because energy can be measured, it is part of the physical world.

Spirit is a little different. It operates on a different dimension. That sounds esoteric, and perhaps it is, but it can't be measured. It isn't "felt" in the body through the senses. It's "felt" on a different level. Spirit can use energy, but it transcends energy.

It's beyond space and time, so it can be in different times and different places at once.

Again, I know this sounds rather opaque. I can't give a clear explanation. However, this is why we accept these concepts as a "mystery." This is a part of the Unknowing.

CHAPTER 60

However, you may ask, "How should it be?" Christ physically went up into the air and sent the Holy Spirit from above, as He said He would, so you think heaven is above you. His disciples witnessed this, and we believe it. So you think, given this evidence, why shouldn't you pray upward?

Since Christ had to rise physically and then send the Holy Spirit physically, it made more sense for it to happen up and from above than down and from below, before or after, on one side or the other. But without this, he wouldn't have needed to go up or down more. To be near the way. Spiritually, heaven and up are equally as close as down and up. Before is like behind. Thus, anyone who wants to be in heaven is there spiritually. Desire, not steps, is the fastest path. St. Paul says this about himself and others: Our bodies are on earth, but our spiritual lives are in heaven. He discussed their spiritual life and love. A soul abides in the object it loves as much as it controls and gives life to its body. So we don't have to push our spirits up, down, or sideways to go to heaven as spirits.

◆ ◆ ◆

Samyama combines the three "upper" practices of yoga—dharana (concentration), dhyana (contemplation), and samadhi (union). They aren't outward, observable practices such as asana (the Western idea of yoga) or pranayama (breath practice). Instead, samyama connects us with the object of our desire.

No, this isn't the Law of Attraction. It allows us to experience connectedness to another person or to God. For example, our typical prayer practice might involve dharana, or concentration.

We focus our minds on God or a virtue of God. The person who prays remains separate from the object—or other.

A dhyana practice moves beyond typical prayer, or concentration, and rests in God or those virtues. The person who prays in this manner begins to feel a two-way communication here. The subject/object relationship becomes less distinct because there is a spiritual connection there.

Although we can't snap into samadhi, we could experience this state for a brief moment. This is where we experience union with God or capture a glimpse of heaven. In other words, heaven isn't necessarily "up there." Instead, it's all around if we purify our desire for it.

The Cloud indicates something similar. Chapter 60 continues explaining that heaven could be "down" just as it could be "up." It's not a destination in a physical sense, but a spiritual one.

Note the emphasis on desire. We must ask ourselves what we really desire. If it's stripped from its substance, it might not be what we believe it to be.

For example, I might desire the love of a certain man. If I practice samyama and begin to concentrate on that desire, I might find that the desire for the man, stripped away from the physical presence, might actually look like the desire for intimacy.

It also might look like something else. I might desire a certain job, which might award me a certain power. If that desire isn't pure, focusing on that power can lead me away from God, even if I'm awarded the job. I might not experience union or heaven because the desire itself pointed me in a different direction. Even a one-degree turn of the tiller can steer the boat way off course.

Our desires can definitely steer our lives in directions we might not have intended. Therefore, we should pay a little more attention to what we truly desire. If we truly desire heaven, we're already there. If we desire something else, we shouldn't be surprised if our soul is fixed on that other target.

CHAPTER 61

Still, we must raise our eyes and hands to the physical heaven where the elements are, but only if our spirit stirs us. If not, we shouldn't care. Physical things are ruled by spiritual things, not vice versa.

Our Lord's ascension illustrates this. Even though He is God, the Holy Spirit enabled Him to go to His Father physically as a man. This was most likely a move upward.

Those who do this book's spiritual work can visualize this body-spirit submission. Because a soul moves him to do this work, the soul works so quickly that he doesn't even realize it. The spirit will straighten the person's body if it was slumping. That's reasonable.

This is why a man's body, the most beautiful thing God made, stands upright rather than facing the earth like other animals. Why? Our bodies should look like the work of the soul, and the spiritual posture is always upright, not crooked. Note that I said the spirit, not the body, is always upright. How could a soul, which is not a body, strain to stand upright? It might not.

Even if it's described as "up or down, in or out, behind or before, on one side or the other," it probably spiritual, not physical. Even if something isn't spiritual, talk about it physically. That's because speech uses the tongue, which is a physical part. So what? Should it be taken literally? No, it might have been meant spiritually.

◆ ◆ ◆

Our physical postures can definitely reflect what's going on in our minds and spirits. If we know someone is looking at us, or if we want someone to look at us, we might change our posture to impress or attract attention. This is our ego saying "Look at me! I'm worthy of being observed." We see this commonly on social media.

Several years ago, I took a workshop with Dharma Mittra, a rather influential yoga teacher. I admired two of his followers who sat by his side. They would sit upright, with eyes closed, while he spoke. I talked with both of them, and they definitely had a peaceful way of being. It was evident to me that they "walked the walk."

Two other followers weren't quite on the path. One spent most of the time taking pictures of him on her phone. She had an inner restlessness that was evident in her mannerisms.

Another one was rather comical to me. At the start of Mittra's first talk, he sat upright in this rather stiff posture. As the talk continued, his posture began to slump. He would arrive the next morning with a "meditation shawl," which is basically a scarf, that he bought at the gift shop. I couldn't help but get the impression that he was all about show and not about substance. He was a sophomore on the path.

When we believe we're being observed or watched, we act differently. Our gestures change, our speech changes, and we carry ourselves differently. We might be a total son-of-a-bitch, but when we're trying to impress others, we change. Again, this is the false self trying to convince others that we are worthy.

During prayer or meditation, particularly after a while, what is our posture? The Cloud says that our physical bodies might grow uncomfortable. Once our ego lets go of its need to have the body look a certain way, the spirit takes over. The spirit then holds our body upright.

This is the key—shedding the layers of the ego/false self so that the spirit can guide us. We get out of our own way and allow the deepest, most essential part of ourselves to steer the ship.

CHAPTER 62

I should tell you what some spiritual words mean so you can better understand how these words spoken out loud can be perceived spiritually. This is so you know when your spiritual work is below you and outside of you, inside you and even with you, and above you and under your God.

Your body is below your soul. The sun, moon, and stars above your body are also below your soul.

Angels and souls are pure and have grace and virtues, making them more wholesome than you, but they are still human.

Mind, Reason, and Will are your soul's main powers. Imagination and senses also matter, but they are secondary.

God is nature's highest.

Spiritual works use "you" to mean your soul. After that, your soul's powers will evaluate everything below, within, and above you.

◆ ◆ ◆

Take a look at most of the messages you see in modern media, including emails, social media posts, and billboards. To engage your attention, they must engage your senses. To continue to keep you hooked on their message, some will engage your imagination. They get you to imagine how you will feel or look if you have this product (or idea) and appeal to your need to belong or your need for power, to name a few.

Most advertising models work this way, using peripheral cues such as an attractive spokesperson or emotional appeals to sell products. Entertainment media, particularly TikTok or YouTube, will arouse your senses without regard for an essential message. Many people find news media "boring" because it doesn't appeal much to the senses or imagination, unless, of course, you tune into the outrageous cable news opinion shows.

When messages appeal to the imagination or the senses, they can be quite influential because they bypass logic and reason. When we consume any media (or product) to arouse the senses, we might be gratified for a moment, but it's not long before we need more sensory gratification again. Even if we buy something on impulse, we feel disappointed later when logic or reason kicks in.

The author of The Cloud writes that the soul has three strong powers—mind (or memory), reason, and will. The imagination and the senses are secondary, meaning that they serve the mind, reason, and will. How often do we get that reversed?

I'm continually reminded of the Katha Upanishad, which describes those who pursue sensory pleasures as missing the goal of life. The senses have the ability to hypnotize us and lead us away from a life of purpose:

> When one lacks discrimination
> And his mind is undisciplined, the senses
> Run hither and thither like wild horses.
> But they obey the rein like trained horses
> When one has discrimination and has made
> The mind one-pointed.[69]

How often do we let the wild horses of our senses and imagination run us way off course? Instead, the senses and imagination can inform the mind, reason, and will. It is then we can make more discerning choices about how to live our lives off our contemplative space.

CHAPTER 63

Mind is so powerful, but it doesn't work by itself. Reason, Will, Imagination, and the Senses work with the Mind, but Mind knows and understands all four powers. The Mind doesn't necessarily work, but instead sorts through these four powers to understand.

Thus, some of a soul's powers are primary and others are secondary. It's not that the soul may be split. Instead, it's because all the things the powers work with are divided into primary (spiritual) and secondary (physical) categories. Reason and Will, the main working powers, work alone in spiritual matters. Imagination and senses work well with all bodily things, present or absent, in the body and physical reality. A soul cannot know the good and bad of physical things, nor why they exist or how they were made, without Reason and Will.

Reason and Will are "principal powers" because they operate in spirit without a body. Imagination and the senses are "secondary powers" because they use the body's five senses. Mind is a main power because it contains all the powers and their components. Let's investigate.

◆ ◆ ◆

The author continues his explanation of the five faculties of mind, reason, will, imagination, and senses, relegating the last two to the physical world. The mind, because it doesn't directly deal with physical reality, integrates information from all these faculties. It can "make sense" of things.

Consider the idiom "out of his mind." This is someone who lacks reason, but perhaps has a strong desire, or will, to act.

Another person might have too much reason, but lack the will to do anything. What might happen if someone lacks reason or will and only reacts through the imagination or the senses? This might be someone under the influence of drugs, only acting through response to what they perceive in the physical world.

Sound confusing? Yep, me too. It's hard to imagine how these faculties could work independently without one another. Ok, perhaps when we're dreaming our imagination works alone, but even psychologists will say that our mind is trying to process things while we dream.

What is interesting here is that The Cloud was written well before the era of modern psychology. Perhaps the author had some training in philosophy, but his ability to distinguish the five faculties of the soul is pretty visionary.

That being said, I can't help but go back to the Hindu texts such as the Upanishads and the Bhagavad Gita, which emphasize how important it was to discipline the mind. The Katha Upanishads would put reason—or the discriminating intellect—above mind.

It recognizes that our thoughts can bounce around our minds, particularly when we are still. God can't speak to us if our minds are darting about. It's up to us—it is our will—to practice settling our thoughts. Once we get out of the way, putting these thoughts of the world into the Cloud of Forgetting, we might see a glimmer of God. Here are the words from the Katha Upanishad:

> He is revealed only
> To those who keep their mind one-pointed
> On the Lord of Love and thus develop
> A superconscious manner of knowing.[70]

It makes sense, doesn't it? If we rely too much on our senses and imagination, we might be easily deluded into believing that God is responsible for something that our ego—or mankind—brought about. The Katha Upanishad says, "Thus we look to the world outside and see not the Self within us." It's impossible to "find" God "out there" through our physical senses. God is found within and beyond our senses and imagination.

CHAPTER 64

Reason is a power that helps us separate the bad from the good, the bad from the worst, the good from the best, the worst from the worst, and the best from the best. Before man sinned, Reason might have done all of this on its own. But now, because of the original sin, it is so blind that it can't do this work unless grace shines a light on it. And both Reason and its object can be understood and held in the Mind.

Will is a power that lets us choose what's good and then make sure it's good. It's also how we love what's good, want what's good, and rest with full liking and agreement in God. Before man sinned, Will could not be tricked in what he chose, who he loved, or what he did. It used to be able to enjoy each thing for what it was, but now it can't do that unless grace upon it. Because of the original sin, people often mistake something that is full of evil for something good, even if it looks good. And both the wish and the thing that is wished for are in the Mind.

❖ ❖ ❖

In so many New Age practices, we're told to get out of thinking and "trust our feeling." Even in self-help programs, we're called to "chase our desires." The Cloud says, "Not so fast." It's clear that many people today are not only out of their minds, but they're also chasing the illusive. The author of The Cloud writes that the power of Reason is especially important because we are incapable of judging what's good or bad without it. Without Reason, our anger or discomfort towards someone might "feel" justified, and we might act on it. However, a brief look into our psychological complexes, projections, and imagoes could easily tell us that those feelings are based on something in our past. In other words, there might be nothing "wrong" with the person. We just believe this because there is something this person elicits within us. Reason will have us pause before we react.

Our Will can be easily deceived without Reason to decide what is good. This often manifests in our disordered desires. When we let our desires run the show, we justify them with certain needs. We "need to belong" or we "need to be heard." Without reason, we might not question why we're so needy. Perhaps these "needs" have us chasing something we have already within us. Reason forces us to grow up and carefully discern before taking action.

We see this too often when people seek to belong to groups that are deceptive. On the surface, these groups might appear benevolent because they use words that pacify our feelings or desires. They know how to hook us. Once we're hooked, they tell us not to trust Reason. They tell us we think too much, and that modern society uses its brain and not its heart.

The Cloud says that our brain, Reason, can be illumined by the grace of God, which will allow us to see things as they are. We ask God for this grace so we can see clearly rather than be blinded by our desires or feelings.

CHAPTER 65

Imagination is a power that lets us see images of both past and present things. Both Imagination and the things it works on are stored in Mind. Before man sinned, the imagination was so obedient to Reason, which it serves, that it never gave Reason an unplanned image of a living creature or a fantasy of a spiritual creature. This is no longer the case, though. Because if it isn't stopped by the light of grace in Reason, it will never stop, whether you're sleeping or awake, to show you random images of physical things or a fantasy that is nothing but a physical idea of a spiritual thing or a spiritual idea of a physical thing. And this is always fake, false, and close to being wrong.

New devotees who have walked away from the world show this Imagination disobedience during prayer. Before the light of grace in Reason restrains the Imagination in a big way, as it does when people constantly think about spiritual things like their own misery, the love and kindness of our Lord God, and many other things, they can't get rid of the wonderful and different thoughts, fantasies, and images that Imagination puts in their minds. All of this disobedience is what hurts because of original sin.

❖ ❖ ❖

The author describes imagination as "disobedient" or "undisciplined" because original sin broke it free from reason. Before original sin, he writes, imagination served as a "handmaid"[71] of reason. Of course, we must remember that this was written when church institutions served as a revered and essential structure in society.

I'm continually fascinated by the imagination of many creatives in this world. Great technological innovations and significant creative works have emerged out of imagination. Therefore, I don't believe that the author contends that imagination is necessarily bad. Because it has shaken loose from reason, it "lends itself increasingly to invention and falsity, leading soon into error."[72]

For an element of the imagination to manifest in reality, such as an innovation or creative work, it must cooperate with reason. A scientist must abide by certain physical laws before challenging them. An artist must commit the work to the proper medium to find its expression in reality. In other words, imagination can only find expression in reality when it concedes to an element of reason.

The author understands that when someone first approaches contemplation, the imagination can easily take the person to the most beautiful and tempting places. This is because in more structured prayer practices, such as reciting the Our Father or praying with a rosary, the imagination is constrained. Because contemplation has little structure, our worldly thoughts feed our imagination and lead us to believe they are real.

We see this in Eastern traditions, where Maya is seen as a force that deceives us into believing our illusions are real. Similarly, Mara is a deity who tempted the Buddha with a variety of sensual temptations to prevent him from achieving enlightenment.

Whether we believe this illusion to be a deity or our worldly temptations running rampant in our imagination, we must remain aware of how it can keep us mired in delusion if it's not tied to reason.

CHAPTER 66

Sensory Perception is a power of our soul that rules and guides our bodily senses. It's how we know and feel all bodily things, whether they make us feel good or bad. And it has two parts: one that serves the needs of our bodies, and another that serves the wants of our bodies. For this is the same power that complains when the body doesn't have what it needs, and when we get what we need, it makes us want to get more than we need to feed and satisfy our lusts. This is the same power that complains when there aren't any pleasing creatures around, but gets excited when there are. This is the same power that complains when there are creatures it doesn't like, but gets excited when they're gone. The Mind holds both our sensory needs and wants.

Before man sinned, Sensory Perception was so subservient to the Will, to which it is almost a servant, that it never gave it any unplanned likes or dislikes from a living creature or any fake likes or dislikes from a dead enemy in a living mind. But that isn't the case anymore. If it isn't ruled by grace in the Will, it won't be able to feel the pain of original sin, which it feels in the absence of needed comforts and in the presence of quick discomforts, and it won't be able to resist lust in the presence of needed comforts and lustful pleasure in the absence of quick discomforts. Instead, it will be like a pig in mud, wallowing in the riches of this world.

◆ ◆ ◆

In many first-world countries, it's easy to indulge. We indulge in excess food, sex, material possessions, and experiences. It's so tempting to leave my chaotic job every once in a while to take a trip to Bali for a "retreat," even though it's not a retreat from our sensory indulgences. The Catholic tradition takes the time of Lent to refrain from a particular indulgence that has gone out of control, and hence it interferes with our ability to live in freedom. In fact, in previous ages, Mardi Gras was the time to rid the household of any substance that would interfere with the Lenten sacrifice. Catholics would refrain from eating in excess during these 40 days.

As a kid, this was always a difficult time. Because we couldn't eat between meals on Fridays, we would always wait until midnight to raid the refrigerator. We didn't understand the purpose of all this fasting and abstinence, especially since we didn't have much devotion to God. We went to church because we had to, and we practiced the rules because we had to. Although many in my community were Catholic, the kids I mostly played with weren't, and these practices didn't seem relevant to a kid that just wants to play Greek dodge and Atari.

However, these practices emphasize the importance of willpower. Just as the power of Reason is superior to Imagination, the power of the Will is superior to the Sensory. Before the fall, the Will kept the senses in line. Without the will, the senses can dart our lives significantly out of control. You don't have to look far to see evidence of how our senses can cause us to act with impulse. The will, let alone reason, never has any time to say, "WAIT!" We've already reached for our phone, that drink, or that pleasure.

It's not to say that desires, or the senses, are bad. The Cloud recognizes the importance of the senses to provide information about the outside world. Our senses can alert us to danger. They also draw us towards connection, perhaps towards intimacy with others. The Cloud also points out the other function of our senses, which is to satisfy an insatiable thirst. This function also causes us to go beyond what the body needs and can result in compulsion, attachment, or addiction. Without the will to redirect this insatiable thirst, we jump on a continuing cycle of want-gratification.

Why do we have this insatiable desire within us? Why are we never satisfied with what we have? Why are we always reaching for more—beyond what the body needs? Why can't we be satisfied with our connections with others? Again, this goes back to the author's contention that after the fall, the mind was blown into disorder, where the powers of the mind fell out of alignment. Eventually, through time, through circumstances, and through awareness, we arrive at a place St. Augustine wrote about thousands of years ago. "You made us for yourself, and our heart is restless until it rests in You."[73]

CHAPTER 67

We've fallen into the kind of misery you can see here because of sin, so it's not surprising that we're easily and blindly fooled by spiritual words and actions, especially from those who don't yet know the power of their souls and how they work.

For as long as the Mind is focused on something physical, even if it is for a good reason, you are below yourself and have no soul. And whenever you feel your Mind thinking about the subtle conditions of your soul's powers and how they work in spiritual things, like vices or virtues, of yourself or of any spiritual creature, or even with you in nature, so that you can learn more about yourself and get closer to perfection, you are within yourself and even with yourself. But when you feel that your mind isn't thinking about anything physical or spiritual, but only the essence of God as it is described in this book, you are above yourself and below your God.

You are better than yourself because you are able to get there through God's grace when you couldn't get there on your own. That is, to be connected to God spiritually, lovingly, and in accordance with his will. You are below your God, even though it can be said in a way that God and you are not two but one in spirit at this time—so much so that you or someone else who feels the perfection of this work can be called a "god" based on what the Bible says[74], but you are still below Him. For He is God by nature, and He has always been God. You, on the other hand, were nothing at one point, and when you were made something by His power and love, you sinned and made yourself worse than nothing. It is only by His grace that you are made a god in grace, joined to Him in spirit without leaving, both here on earth and in heaven. So, even though you have the same grace as God, you are still much lower than God in nature.

Here, you can get an idea of how easy it is for someone who doesn't know their own soul's powers and how they work to be tricked into thinking they understand words that are written with a spiritual purpose. So you can see why I didn't tell you straight out to tell God what you wanted. Instead, I told you to act like a child, which is to hide it and cover it up. And I do this because I don't want you to think literally what I meant spiritually.

◆ ◆ ◆

Is it any wonder that most of the time, we are out of our minds? When we don't understand how the mind has become disordered, we easily slip into disarray. The author writes that when we're focused on something in the physical world, which for the ordinary person is almost always, we're considered "beneath" ourselves. When we're in recollection or introspection, that is, reflecting on spiritual matters, we're "within" ourselves. The whole point of the work of contemplation is to transcend ourselves, to go beyond ourselves. Even then, as we are "one with God in spirit and in love and in the oneness of wills,"[75] we're still beneath God in this union.

I've seen some modern Eastern gurus who claim to be God. I won't mention them here because they've accrued quite a following here in the United States rather than in the East. Why the U.S.? My guess is the desire for power. We seek to be more powerful than God, often putting false idols such as social status or money in the place of God. Or perhaps we might also believe in God, yet we still want to worship the powers that hold together the material world. We can't worship two.[76]

This confusion might result from reading things out of context. For instance, we might read, "[Y]ou or any person who by such an act of unification has reached the perfection of this work may certainly on the testimony of Scripture be called a God."[77] Our hearts leap with this, and maybe we'll create a social media meme using this quote. But remember, God precedes us always, and the Cloud reminds us that we're never equal with

God. Even Jesus, "who, as He already existed in the form of God, did not consider equality with God something to be grasped,"[78] emptied himself so that he could serve humankind. In other words, he didn't use his divinity to control others or to tempt others to have the powers of God. Instead, we assume the same posture of service, which means giving up any means of personal gain.

This means putting Reason and Will back in the proper order, with the imagination and senses serving them.

CHAPTER 68

If someone else told you to gather all of your powers and wits inside of yourself and worship God there, even if they said it was true and no one could be more true, I wouldn't tell you to do it out of fear that they were lying or that their words would make you think of something else. But this is what I will say. Don't go so deep within yourself that you become too deeply immersed in your small self. I also advise not to be above, behind, or one side or the other of yourself.

"Then where shall I be?" you asked. "It seems you want me to be nowhere." Now, you're right, that's where I'd like to have you. You might be nowhere physically, but you'll be everywhere spiritually. Look hard to make sure that your spiritual work is nowhere physically. Then, wherever that thing is that you deliberately work on in your mind, you are there in spirit, just as your body is there where you are physically. And even if your physical desires to be somewhere else, persevere spiritually because you love God. So, don't worry about those desires, but work hard with a strong desire to have God without anyone else knowing. For I tell you the truth, I'd rather be so physically nowhere and fight with that blind nothing than be such a great lord that I could be physically everywhere and play with all that I own.

Compare this everywhere and this nothing. Don't worry about it if you can't figure out what it means, because I love it much more. It is too good to justify. This nothing is better felt than seen, because it is completely blind and dark to those who have only just looked at it. Still, if I were to be more precise, I would say that a soul is more blinded by a lot of spiritual light than by darkness or a lack of body light. Who is he who says it doesn't matter? It must be our outer man, not our inner man. Our inner self calls it "All," because he has learned enough about it to know the reason for everything, living or dead, without paying special attention to any one thing on its own.

◆ ◆ ◆

I had been describing how contemplation had significantly been feeding my spiritual life. My bible study group had been meeting on Zoom, which was hardly the best medium for interpersonal dialogue. One of the women in my group—who was very disciplined in her prayer practice—was skeptical.

"What do you think about when you're sitting there in contemplation?"

"Nothing," I said.

"That's not Catholic," she said. "That's dangerous. That's how evil gets in."

She continued to describe her own journey in yoga, New Age, and meditation. For her, it was a "dark" time in her life. It took her to some uncomfortable places.

I completely understand. Spiritual work can be dark. Without a strong foundation, you can go in the wrong direction. You can be led down a path that leads to more hedonism or more affliction because it's rooted in the outer, false self rather than the inner, spiritual self.

It's not to say that these practices always lead down the wrong path. Many people can navigate through this path and discern what is genuine. They are grounded through reason and pure will, and their motives aren't selfish. They don't want to attain enlightenment so that they can win approval, achieve success, or obtain prosperity. They're looking for meaning so that they can live more compassionately in the world.

The Cloud doesn't promise enlightenment. It doesn't promise anything. It's not an instruction manual. It's somewhat descriptive of the path, but it cannot describe what union is like. It concedes that it "cannot be explained, only experienced."[79]

The outer self perceives it to be "nowhere." It feels rather empty because it's beyond our perception. However, deep within, the Cloud says, it is "everywhere and all." It's a fullness beyond measure.

For someone beginning this path, this might seem esoteric. For someone who prefers active practices, like the woman in my bible study, this might never be understood. Some people are uncomfortable with the inscrutable, and that's fine.

Many might be turned off by The Cloud because it seems really confusing. I was one of those people many years ago. It's like trying to explain a college concept to someone in kindergarten. I just didn't have the foundation.

Similarly, the path of yoga doesn't start with samadhi. It starts with cleaning up how you behave towards others, then how you take care of yourself. You then work physically to iron out and open up some of those issues that you were afraid to address. You breathe through some of the issues to help you process them effectively. Very slowly, you tune within. You begin to focus less on what's going on "out there" and train to focus on what's inside. Eventually, you go beyond that, too.

The practice of mindfulness is effective in those middle stages because it helps dissolve some heavily charged issues. Many times, your mind will ruminate over a negative episode, trying to replay it or relive it differently. It will also rehearse things that haven't happened. Mindfulness directs our attention to what the body is doing right now, right here. It develops concentration in the mind and gets us out of the dangerous, traumatic episodes that keep us stuck.

This present-moment awareness is effective in the journey, particularly when we're emotionally charged or mentally stressed. This "I'm here" awareness, though, is only a preparation for samadhi or contemplation. Eventually the "now here" turns to "nowhere." We learn to let go of being "within ourselves" and transcend this "self."

Mindfulness is concerned with drawing the mind to the body, which is certainly important. However, we enter into a new space spiritually when the mind softens around its worldly turmoil and focuses on God alone.

CHAPTER 69

A man's love is wonderfully different in how he feels about this nothing when it's nowhere made. Because when a soul looks at it for the first time, it will see all the sins it has done since it was born, whether they were done in the flesh or as a spirit, in the light or in the dark. And no matter how he turns it, they will always be in front of his eyes, until the time comes when much hard work, many painful sighs, and many bitter tears have washed away a lot of them. Sometime during this trouble, he thinks that looking at it is like looking at hell, and he thinks that he will never be able to get perfect spiritual rest from it. So far inwards come many people, but because they feel a lot of pain and don't have any comfort, they turn around and look at physical things again, looking for physical comforts outside because they haven't yet earned spiritual ones, which they would have if they had stayed.

For the person who stays feels some comfort and has some hope of being perfect, because he feels and sees that a lot of his forgiven sins are being washed away by God's grace. Even so, he still feels pain, but he thinks it will end because the pain is getting less and less. So, he doesn't call it anything else but purgatory. Sometimes he can't find a specific sin written on it, but he still thinks sin is a lump. He doesn't know what the lump is, but he thinks it's him. This could be called the base and the pain of the original sin. He sometimes thinks it's paradise or heaven because of all the wonderful sweetness, comfort, joy, and good things he finds there. He sometimes thinks of it as God because it gives him peace and rest.

He can think whatever he wants. Between him and his God, there will always be a cloud of unknowing.

❖ ❖ ❖

As we near closer to the end of The Cloud, the author describes something similar to the *noche oscura*--the dark night—described by St. John of the Cross. Most of the book leads us toward the mouth of this cave, but this chapter tells us that it feels like hell. It's natural for him to wait until the end of the text to describe it—otherwise, so many would be turned off by it.

Throughout the text, we've seen many references to our sinfulness. Let's face it, this is what's missing in many New Age approaches. Rather than recognize where we've made mistakes and make course corrections, we make efforts to glaze over them or forget them, even though the essence within us that caused us to sin is still there. It always will be. We must always walk with awareness as we move through life because the moment we're unconscious, we're easily led toward worldly temptations.

Once we're led to the place of "nowhere," which seems rather empty, the Cloud says that we're made more aware of our sinful behaviors. At this point in our spiritual lives, we might believe we're indeed living the "good" life, free from the temptation of sin. In this "nowhere," though, "No evil thought, word, or deed remains hidden."[80] We have no place to hide here. Moments we might have chosen to forget, such as the way we treated a person when we were 11 years old, bubble up. We don't think we're worth it.

Although St. John of the Cross doesn't mention turning away from this place of nothingness, The Cloud says that many people will backslide because it can be difficult to bear.

St. John calls this "aridity," and it indeed requires a certain patience and strength. If we continue to choose to flee from ourselves, we will definitely flee from this. We return to those old places that gave us temporary gratification until we're ready to take it up again.

I know for myself this happened. I began to enter the dark night, this place of nowhere, in my mid-30s. I began to experience that beautiful stillness, and it attracted me to walk further. Then I arrived at a juncture where I could experience the aridity or explore a new life of physical pleasures. I chose the physical, spending the next decade or so competing in triathlons and bodybuilding competitions. I wasn't yet willing to face myself.

Eventually, though we get burned out of that. God offers us another chance, and perhaps this time, we take it. According to The Cloud, we learn that this "hell" that we feel we're experiencing is a purifying fire like that of purgatory.

Although we might still feel our sins as a "lump" to keep us humble, we also notice that, by the grace of God, are sins are forgiven. We begin to experience small glimpses of consolation, of union. We no longer want to go back to our old ways.

CHAPTER 70

So, work hard at this "nothing" and "nowhere," and leave your "outer body wits" and all the things they do, because I promise you that your outer self can't comprehend it.

You can't imagine anything with your eyes unless you know its length and width, how big or small it is, whether it's round or square, how far or close it is, and what color it is. And you can imagine nothing beyond noise or some kind of sound in your ears. By your nose, nothing but smell or taste. And everything is either sour or sweet, salty or fresh, bitter or pleasing to your taste. And everything you feel is either hot or cold, hard or soft, sharp or smooth. And really, neither God nor spirits have any of these things or amounts. So, leave your physical senses alone and don't use them to do anything, either inside or outside. Those who set them up to be spiritual workers inside and hope to hear, smell, see, taste, or feel spiritual things, whether inside or outside, will be fooled and will be going against the flow of nature.

Because they were made that way by nature, people can only use the physical senses to learn about physical things and can't use them to learn about spiritual things. I mean by what the senses are meant to do. By their shortcomings, we can know that some things we read or hear about are not real. For example, if we read or hear about something and think that our senses can't tell us what it is, we can be sure that it is something spiritual and not physical.

In the same way, it seems strange to our spiritual minds when we try to figure out how to know God. Even if a person has a lot of spiritual understanding and knows about all made spiritual things, he will never be able to understand an unmade spiritual thing, which is nothing but God. But it could fail because the thing it fails at is

God. And that's why St. Denis said that the best way to know God is to know what you don't know. And anyone who reads Denis's books will find that his words clearly back up everything I've said or will say in this treatise, from the beginning to the end. On anything but this, neither he nor any other doctor can help me right now. For a long time, people thought it was weak to say nothing that came from their own minds unless it was confirmed by the Bible or a doctor. Now, people do it out of curiosity and to show how smart they are. It doesn't matter to you, so I won't do it. For whoever has ears, let him hear, and whoever is moved to sow, let him sow, because if they don't, they won't.

◆ ◆ ◆

Many people don't believe in God because they want evidence. They want to perceive God with the senses. They want to hear God, see God, or feel God. This is logical, given many of the things they know and understand about the world comes from the senses. Because they eschew authoritarianism, they want to experience God for themselves. I understand that.

On the other hand, others rely too much on the senses, particularly "feeling" their emotions manifest in the body. They believe that this is the evidence of God. When we feel our chest heating up, we trust that emotional response as a sign from God.

Neither is the case with God. Because God is spiritual, God cannot be experienced in the senses. Sure, we can experience God in the creation and appreciate Him in awe. But God's creation is not God. Otherwise, we would be worshipping ourselves, because we, too, are God's creation. And yes, so is that asshole politician.

As in previous chapters, The Cloud alludes to pratyahara, the work of withdrawing cues from the senses. Some yoga practitioners take this literally and close off their noses and ears. We do this metaphorically by directing our attention within. We do our best to ignore our sensory distractions, such as the snoring dog or the smell of fresh bread. We can acknowledge them for a moment rather than become irritated at their presence, but then we return to our inwardly-drawn concentration.

This is why contemplation doesn't come easy. When we're tempted and continually aroused by the senses, they become dull. They don't notice subtle changes. Sometimes these subtle changes are warnings that something bigger is coming. The senses serve as ways for us to perceive the physical world so that we can navigate through it. However, they don't give us much understanding of the spiritual world. We can't use physical properties to describe God. As The Cloud writes, we can't say God has a certain smell or sound. We might have certain metaphors from the physical world to describe God, but they are only representations, not God. On the other hand, "when we read or hear of certain things and realize that our outward senses cannot tell us what the qualities of these things may be, we can be quite sure then that those things are spiritual things and are not physical things."[81]

Similarly, people cannot describe enlightenment. Any description of enlightenment isn't enlightenment, but imagination. They just know that it's something they experienced in spirit. It goes beyond knowledge, which is called The Cloud of Unknowing.

"When we reach the end of what we know, that's where we find God."[82]

CHAPTER 71

Some people think this matter is so hard and scary that it can't be reached without a lot of hard work beforehand, and it can only be thought of very rarely, and only when the heart is full. And to these men, I'll answer as delicately as I can by saying that it's all God's will and plan, based on how strong their souls are, that gives them the ability to think and work through spirits.

Some people can't get there without a lot of and long-term spiritual practice, but they won't feel the perfection of this work until they get a special calling from our Lord. This calling is called "ecstasy." Some people are so humble in spirit and grace, and so at home with God in this grace of contemplation, that they can have it whenever they want, whether they are sitting, walking, standing, or kneeling. Still, they can use all of their minds at this time if they want to.

Moses is a good example of the first, and Aaron, who was a priest in the Temple, is a good example of the second. This is because the Ark of the Covenant in the old law represents the grace of contemplation, and the people who work in this grace represent those who worked with the Ark the most, as the story will show. And it's true that this grace and this work are like the Ark. For just as that Ark held all the jewels and relics of the Temple, this little love on this cloud holds all the good qualities of a person's soul, which is the spiritual Temple of God.

Before Moses could see the Ark and find out how it was made, he had to work very hard to get to the top of the mountain, where he stayed and worked in a cloud for six days. He stayed there until the seventh day, when God agreed to show him how to make the Ark. By Moses's long work, people can see that they can't finish this spiritual work without putting in a lot of work first, and that God will only show it to them when he's ready.

But because Aaron was in charge, he could let Moses see it in the Temple behind the Veil as often as he liked. This was because Moses could only come see it rarely and only after a lot of hard work. And by this Aaron, I mean all of the people I talked about above, who, with the help of grace and their spiritual smarts, can finish this work in whatever way they want.

◆ ◆ ◆

Some might be aware of the story of the Buddha, who was first a prince, but then would abandon his life of wealth and privilege to live in austerity. Although he had learned how to discipline his mind from the great teachers of his time, it wasn't until he sat under a bodhi tree for six days that the light came on.

Muhammad, the father of Islam, wasn't rich, but he was devoted to his faith. He would take many trips to a small mountain cave for prayer. When he was about 40 years old, the angel Gabriel visited him with the message that "God is one."

Stories similar to this are told in the Bible. We learn about the struggles of Abraham, Joseph, Moses, and Job. All faced significant struggles before they would hear from God.

We must wonder—is all that struggle necessary to hear from God? Why should I endure all this hardship and austerity to receive a brief moment of ecstasy? Isn't prayer supposed to be simple? Why is contemplation considered "work?"

The author of The Cloud uses the story of Moses to explain. In Exodus 24, Moses climbed Mount Sinai, which was covered in a thick cloud for several days. Then God spoke to Moses from the cloud, giving him instructions about the Ark of the Covenant, the Tabernacle, and the Ten Commandments.

The author writes that Moses endured significant hardship and eventually received a revelation (he calls it "ecstasy") from God. This isn't always the case, and people like this are rare. For Aaron, who was consecrated as a priest, it didn't take arduous work. He "had it in his power to see God in the temple behind the veil as often as he liked to go in."[83]

How we might receive the gift of contemplation depends on our spiritual capacity and God's will. Some are like Moses, who must endure hardships to hear profound messages from God. It's also important to note that this gift isn't earned. It's not that if we endure many hardships and sacrifices we will win the affection of God. God chooses some people for this work, and if they endure it, it's not like they are looking for a reward. They understand their work is solely for God. Therefore, their names echo for eternity.

Aaron, on the other hand, represents those people who are already rather discerning about the work of God. They might not receive profound revelations like Moses, but their contemplative experience is a bit more moderate. Rather than experience an ecstatic state on rare occasions, their experience is more ordinary, with "full command of all their faculties, bodily and spiritual, and can use them if they so wish."[84]

If we engage in the work of contemplation desiring these ecstasies, it might take a significant amount of time and hardship. Whether we climb a mountain, enter a cave, or sit under a bodhi tree, the revelation only comes if God chooses. If we desire the ecstasies above desiring God, they might not come until we abandon the desire for ecstasy. If we simply desire God and remain open to his will, our experience might be quite ordinary, but no less important.

CHAPTER 72

Here you can see that a person who can't see and feel the completion of this work without a lot of hard effort can be easily fooled if he tells other people what he feels in himself, which is that they can't get there without a lot of hard work and yet it's still rare. And in the same way, he who can have it whenever he wants can be tricked if he thinks everyone else can have it whenever they want. Let it be. For maybe, if it's like God, those who couldn't get it the first time or only got it after a lot of trouble will be able to get it whenever they want and as often as they want after that. We have Moses as an example of this. At first, he could only see the shape of the Ark on the mountain very rarely and only after a lot of hard work. After that, he could see it whenever he wanted.

◆ ◆ ◆

When I took that "course" on The Cloud, and I was quite taken aback by the idea that contemplation comes easily to anyone. It didn't require much work at all. It was just a matter of getting away from ourselves—forgetting ourselves—and desiring God alone. It also didn't require any lifestyle practices. You could easily infer that you could be a rich politician who continually lies to the public and be able to achieve contemplation.

Words like that can be deceptive. If we frame contemplation as accessible to anyone at any time without a need to shape our lives following God, people could be easily deceived. As was previously mentioned in other chapters, our pride or desire for power could convince us that we're in a contemplative state. We could then proceed to write books about this wild, mystical experience when all the while it's just greed and pride doing their bidding. Then contemplation becomes hypocrisy. After all, why would someone want to live a life of humility and compassion when others live lives of luxury and excess and experience the same thing?

In this chapter, the author warns those contemplatives not to judge their experience as the "only" way. In other words, if someone practices incredible spiritual discipline to achieve the mystical experience, it doesn't mean that everyone has to follow that path. In the same way, if another person experiences contemplation—not necessarily the mystical experience—in the everyday, it doesn't mean others can.

Mind you, the author was assuming that those reading about contemplation were already living life through the church. It was assumed that the author was a monk and perhaps writing to a fellow monk. They were living in accord with the sacraments of the Catholic Church, which meant communal prayer, the Eucharist, and contrition for sins.

It's not like someone who is looking for a mystical experience could pick up The Cloud and say, "Cool! I want to do this!" This someone must have the desire to know God and forsake living according to the rules of the material world. Our attachments to worldly desires will always interfere with our contemplative experience. How much we give up will open our spiritual eyes to what God might have in store for us.

CHAPTER 73

Most of the time, Moses, Bezaleel, and Aaron were the ones who worked with the Ark of the Covenant. Moses learned how to make it on the Mount of Our Lord. Bezaleel made it in the valley, just like the model that was shown in the mountain. Aaron kept it in the Temple so he could touch it and look at it whenever he wanted.

At the same time as these three, this grace of contemplation helps us in three ways. Sometimes we only benefit from God's grace, and when that happens, we're like Moses, who, despite all the climbing and hard work he did to get to the top of the mountain, only saw it a few times. Even then, he only saw it when the Lord showed him, not because of how hard he worked. Sometimes we get this grace through our own spiritual ingenuity, with God's help, and then we're compared to Bezaleel, who couldn't see the Ark until he'd made it himself, with the help of the example that God showed Moses on the mountain. And sometimes we learn about this grace from what other people say, and then we're like Aaron, who was used to being able to see and touch the Ark whenever he wanted, which Bezaleel had built and made ready before his hands.

Look, my spiritual friend, in this work, even though it's written in a childish and rudimentary way, I do the work of Bezaleel, even though I'm a wretch who doesn't deserve to teach anyone anything. I make and explain to your hands how this spiritual Ark is made. But if you want to be Aaron, you can work much better and more worthily than I do. That is, you can always work there for both you and me. Do that, I beg you, for the love of God Most High. And since God has called us both to work on this project, I ask you to do what I can't do for the love of God.

❖ ❖ ❖

Although the author describes two contemplative paths in chapter 71, he describes three in chapter 73. The first was that of Moses, who labored for a long while before he would receive the gift. The author notes, though, that the gift of contemplation wasn't a reward for his work, but given freely. I guess perhaps there was some interior work that needed to be done within him before he could be open to receive. His work was a means of preparation for him to become a great leader in his nation. He needed to endure the work to strengthen his soul for his arduous journey. In this instance, the gift of contemplation is received solely by grace.

As before, he also mentions Aaron. Unless you've read the many stories of the Old Testament, you might not be aware of Aaron's role in caring for the Ark of the Covenant. He was a consecrated priest, so he trusted the authority and teaching of God. He therefore could enter the holiest of holies as he wished. Similarly, those who live spiritually disciplined lives might experience a glimpse of contemplation more frequently. Their lives are much more in order as their hearts are devoted to God. Perhaps God doesn't plan for people like Aaron to liberate the people of Israel from Egypt, so the labor of Moses is not placed upon Aaron. His role to keep order and instruction was important as well but didn't necessitate climbing the mountain.

The author then mentions the third path likened to Bezaleel. Who is that? Going back to Exodus, Bezaleel was the chief architect of the Ark of the Covenant. According to Exodus 31:3, God "filled him with the Spirit of God, with wisdom, with understanding, with knowledge and with all kinds of skills…" Bezaleel already had great gifts as a craftsman, and God used these gifts to create the sacred tabernacle. The fusion of his talent and God's breath of grace represent the third contemplative path.

This is not to say that Moses, Aaron, and Bezaleel were

contemplatives. For some, the gift of contemplation might come while enduring significant hardship. Like Moses, a mystical ecstasy might occur rarely through the grace of God. However, this isn't to be taken lightly, because the message given might be significantly profound. For others, contemplation comes through the benefit of the work of others. Like Aaron being able to enter the tabernacle freely, those who adorn the spiritual garments given to them receive the gift of contemplation more freely. And yet, there is still a third path, which blends our natural talents with God's grace. Moses had described the tabernacle to Bezaleel, but his vision, helped by God's stirring, constructed the magnificent Ark of the Covenant.

The author likens himself to a bad example of Bezaleel because he has the vision of contemplation in his head, but he's unable to construct an adequate description so that his novice could teach (like Aaron) to others.

CHAPTER 74

And if you think that this way of working doesn't fit with your body and soul, you can leave it and try something else, as long as you get good advice from spirits. Then, I beg you to forgive me, because I really wanted to help you with this letter through my simple knowledge. So, read it over twice or three times. The more times you read it, the better it is and the more you will understand it. So much so that maybe a sentence that was really hard for you on your first or second read will seem easy to you soon after.

Indeed, it seems impossible to me that a soul that is interested in this work would read it, speak it, or hear it read or spoken, unless that soul felt at that time that it was having the effect that it was meant to have. Then, if you think it helped you, thank God from the bottom of your heart and, for God's sake, pray for me.

So, do that. And I ask you for the love of God that you don't let anyone see this book, unless it's someone you think is like the book. After that, you'll find written in the book before what men should work on this work and when they should do it. And if you let any of these men see it, please tell them to take their time and look it over carefully. For there might be something in the beginning or the middle that isn't fully said as it stands. But if it isn't there, it will be soon or at the end. So, if a person only saw one part, he might be easily led astray, so I ask you to do what I say. And if you think there is something there that you would like to be more clear than it is, tell me what it is and what you think about it. If I can, I will change it with my simple intelligence.

I didn't care if quarrelsome people, suck-ups and faultfinders, scammers and babblers, and other critics saw this book, because I never meant to write such a thing to them. So, I didn't want them to hear it, nor did I want any of these strangely educated or uneducated people to hear it, even if they were good men who lived an active life. It doesn't fit them.

◆ ◆ ◆

As I was reading the introductions to various interpretations and translations of *The Cloud of Unknowing*, I couldn't help but laugh at one, who criticized another quite harshly. I thought of the Indian parable of the blind men, who never encountered an elephant. Because each was touching different parts of the animal, each interpreted the elephant to be something different from the entirety of the elephant. Although their descriptions were accurate from where they were standing, none could make an accurate account of the whole.

The author of *The Cloud* gives his account of contemplation according to his standpoint within the Catholic Church in the 14th century. Even he admits that contemplation is inscrutable. That's why I find it funny for various interpreters to criticize others. Unless you were talking to the author himself, who remains a mystery, none of these "blind men" can offer the definitive explanation of what the author intended.

The best we can do is read these different translations and interpretations, similar to doing the same with the Bible, and ponder the mystery. Similar to what the author of *The Cloud* tells us, we must accept that some things cannot be definitive. We must put what we know into the cloud of forgetting and be open to something that's beyond our limited minds. We cannot know God through knowledge, and we certainly can't know as much as God. We must also be open to the possibility that our interpretation might not be wholly accurate. It's an interpretation, which might have validity but cannot be "proven" right or wrong. Even in science, there's always room for error.

This chapter in *The Cloud* reiterates that the text must be read in its entirety. Indeed, one part explains others and really cannot be pulled out of context. It bothers me that I took a "course" on *The Cloud* and it never moved beyond Chapter 8. Sure, it was interesting hearing a different perspective on certain concepts, but it didn't elucidate much about *The Cloud*.

The author also knows that reading his text might be confusing at first, so he invites us to read it more than once. Although I've read certain chapters of this text several times throughout my 15 or so years with it, I've read it in its entirety five times. The first time I found it to be stuffy and hard to hear how much of a "wretch" I was. So I put it down for about five years. Each time you pick it up, it speaks to you differently.

A big question is—what draws you to contemplation? The author writes that if this type of prayer doesn't resonate with you, give the book to someone who might be called to it. Some people are very comfortable with their prescribed prayers and rituals and aren't suited to contemplation. Some are committed to their active lives and are suspicious of those contemplatives. The author writes that he hoped that the actives who want to criticize contemplatives would never read his book. Because this book is meant to describe and encourage those called to contemplation, those who want to criticize will not have the eyes to see it clearly.

CHAPTER 75

Not all those who want to practice contemplation because they feel good when they read this book will be called by God to do this work. For maybe this stirring has more to do with the natural curiosity of wit than with a calling from God.

But if they want to find out where this stirring is coming from, they can do it this way. First, they should check to see if they have already cleaned their conscience in accord with the Holy Church. If that's the case, that's fine. If they want to pursue further, they should check to see if contemplation is always on their minds more than any other spiritual activity. And if they think that nothing they do, in the flesh or in the spirit, is enough to satisfy their conscience, unless this secret little love pressed is the most important thing they do, then this is a sign that they were called by God to do this work and nothing else.

I don't mean that it will last forever and always be on the minds of those who are called to carry out this work. Nay, so is it not. In this work, the actual feeling of a young spiritual apprentice is often taken away for different reasons. Sometimes their pride will assume they can have this deep contemplative experience whenever they want. And every time the feeling of grace is taken away, pride is to blame. Not the pride that is there, but the pride that would be there if this feeling of grace wasn't taken away. And this is how some young fools come to think that God is their enemy, even though He is actually their best friend.

Sometimes it's taken away because they weren't careful, and when that happens, they feel a very bitter pain that beats them very hard. Sometimes, our Lord will use a clever technique to make it take longer. This is because He wants it to grow and be more delicate when it is found again after being lost for a long time. And this is one of the best ways to tell if a person is called or not to work in this work: if he feels that after a long delay and lack of this work, when it comes suddenly and for no reason, he wants to labor in this work more than ever before. So much so that I often think that he is happier when he finds it than he was when he lost it.

And if that's the case, it's a sure sign that God has called him to do this work, no matter who or what he is or has been.

Because God doesn't see you for what you are or what you have been, but for what you want to be. And St. Gregory testified that all holy desires grow with time, and if they fade with time, they were never holy desires to begin with. For he who feels less and less joy in new discoveries and sudden manifestations of his old desires, even if they are good and natural desires, they were never holy desires. St. Augustine talks about this holy desire and says that a good Christian man's whole life is nothing but holy desire.

Goodbye, spiritual friend, with God's and my blessings! And I pray to the All-Powerful God that true peace, holy counsel, spiritual comfort in God, and a lot of grace always be with you and all the people who love God on earth. Amen.

◆ ◆ ◆

What calls us to contemplation? Is it a curiosity or a calling? I admit, my initial interest in The Cloud was curiosity that wanted to know more about other types of prayers aside from the structured prayers of the Catholic Church. Many of those prayers didn't feed me so much. I also couldn't do much praying like those of the evangelicals and Pentecostals. I honestly didn't know how to pray. So many of my prayers were complaining about an ex-boyfriend and wondering why someone like me would fall for someone like him. The Cloud—and Centering Prayer—gave me the ability to put all that rumination on pause.

After a while, though, other things took over my life. I still did Centering Prayer, but that, too, left my life. Contemplation returned to me when over and over I asked, "How did people before Jesus pray? How did Jesus pray?" I pictured Anna, who was present in the temple when Mary and Joseph presented Jesus, praying night and day. What prayers was she saying?

Because my head was so filled with the turbulence of my job woes, the only "praying" I could do was sitting in silence. I couldn't pray Ignatian Contemplation because my head was too tired to imagine anything. I just wanted rest.

That's how I see contemplation now—not as much "work," as indicated in The Cloud, but "rest."

Because The Cloud was written by a Catholic monk, he encourages readers to discern between curiosity and calling by first checking our conscience. Those who aren't Catholic might not feel inclined to go to confession, but it is important to question how we're living our lives. Is there something we're hiding that is interfering with our spiritual path? We might not feel inclined to confess it to a priest or a spiritual director, but deep down, God knows. When I'm struggling with how my life is unfolding—like what's going on now—I'm continually asking how I might be getting in my own way. What behaviors am I engaging in that pull me away from God?

This is why having structures in place set forth by a religious tradition are helpful. The yoga tradition has particular observances and disciplines that are very similar to religious traditions. Two of these are quite common in everyone—truth and idol worship. Many times, we can't see what's in front of us because "our truth" gets in the way of THE truth. We invest too heavily in our beliefs rather than accept the possibility that these beliefs are not founded in truth.

Similarly, our attraction to material possessions and certain people can interfere with our spiritual path. Some can form addictions or obsessions, which put them at the forefront of our minds. Our minds cannot have two aims--we can only concentrate on one thing. Because a physical pleasure or a cunning person can be observed with the senses, they can easily take the place of God in our hearts and minds.

Whether we're a part of the Catholic Church or not, the

draw of contemplation must be rooted in the desire for God alone. Sure, it might originally stem from our desire to pray in a different way than what we were originally taught. It might come as a means of personal defiance against our religious upbringing. God finds a way to call us somehow. However, we must continually investigate our desires and motivations to ensure that pride or greed doesn't steer us off the path.

We might "try" contemplative practices for a while and abandon them if they don't bear the fruit we desire. Eventually, if God intends it for us, he will find a way to call us back.

So I leave you friends with the the hope that you will put all distractions into the Cloud of Forgetting and continue to pierce the Cloud of Unknowing.

I pray that wherever you are on the contemplative path, you will always keep your heart open to where God is leading you. Keep the faith. God is always with you on the path.

NOTES

[1] Progoff, p. 27-28
[2] Johnston, The Mysticism of The Cloud of Unknowing, p. 266
[3] Wolters, p. 46
[4] Johnston, p. 46
[5] Billy, p. 33
[6] Thich Nhat Hanh, p. 31
[7] Johnston, p. 47
[8] Johnston, p. 50.
[9] Johnston, p. 54
[10] Johnston, p. 54
[11] London, p. 29
[12] Easwaran, Loc. 659
[13] St. Ignatius was born in 1491, which is about the time when The Cloud of Unknowing was written.
[14] The Etymology of Passion
[15] Billy, p. 68
[16] Billy, p. 71
[17] Butcher, p. 43
[18] Tummo
[19] Rahula
[20] This is interesting because the Billy text is based on the Underhill translation.
[21] The Chosen and two other films have illustrated this idea.
[22] Seneca, pp. 1-2
[23] Trappist Brothers and Sisters
[24] Johnston, p. 74
[25] This also emphasizes the importance of reading different

translations. Although the Acevedo Butcher text is very readable and contemporary, it conflates Mary Magdalene and Mary of Bethany. Because Acevedo Butcher is an English/Medieval Studies scholar and not a Biblical scholar, this could explain this error.

[26] Johnston, p. 74

[27] Letter to the Bishops

[28] Luke 10:42

[29] Romans 8:31

[30] Acts 5:38-39

[31] It's important to note that Jesus didn't speak English—more than likely it was Aramaic. D.J. Billy points out that the author of The Cloud more than likely read the Latin text of the Bible, which uses the term "optimam," which is translated as "best."

[32] Acevedo Butcher, p. 61.

[33] Bernstein and Sharf

[34] Johnston, p. 79

[35] London, p. 50

[36] Read more at Kobell

[37] Johnston, p. 83

[38] Johnston, p. 84

[39] Johnston, p. 84

[40] Letter to the Bishops

[41] Johnston, p. 91

[42] "Poverty of Spirit"

[43] Johnston, p. 93

[44] London, p. 67

[45] Acevedo Butcher, pp. 94-95

[46] Letter to the Bishops

[47] Wolters, p. 106

[48] Johnston, p. 98

[49] Walsh, pp. 197-198

[50] 1 Thessalonians 5:17

[51] Wolters, p. 109

[52] Wolters, p. 110

[53] Johnston, p. 103

[54] Wolters, p. 112

[55] Wolters, p. 111
[56] London, p. 74
[57] Progoff, p. 165
[58] Acevedo Butcher, p. 111
[59] Wolters, p. 115
[60] Progoff, p. 170
[61] "Berakhot 60B:13."
[62] St. John of the Cross uses this analogy in Dark Night of the Soul.
[63] Wolters, p. 121
[64] Walsh, p. 219
[65] Newberg
[66] See Matthew 23
[67] This is often a euphemism to denounce rights for the LGBTQ community.
[68] Revelation 1:16
[69] Easwaran, The Upanishads, p. 81
[70] Easwaran, The Upanishads, p. 82
[71] W. Johnston, p. 132
[72] Progoff, p. 216
[73] St. Augustine, p. 3
[74] John 10:34
[75] Walsh, p. 249
[76] Matthew 6:24
[77] Progoff, p. 221
[78] Philippians 2:6
[79] Johnston, p. 136
[80] Johnston, p. 137
[81] Progoff, p. 229
[82] Acevedo Butcher, p. 174.
[83] Wolters, p. 147
[84] Walsh, p. 258

WORKS CITED

"Berakhot 60B:13." *Sefaria*, https://www.sefaria.org/Berakhot.60b.13?lang=bi.

Bernstein, Alon, and Isaac Scharf. "Mary Magdalene Was Not a Prostitute, Scholars Say. This Is What She Really Was." *The Independent*, Independent Digital News and Media, 1 Apr. 2019, https://www.independent.co.uk/news/world/middle-east/mary-magdalene-feminism-metoo-jesus-disciples-apostle-christianity-judaism-pope-francis-vatican-a8281731.html.

Billy, Dennis Joseph. *The Cloud of Unknowing: A Contemporary Guide to the 14th-Century Classic*. Liguori Publications, 2014.

Butcher, Carmen Acevedo. *The Cloud of Unknowing*. Shambhala Publications, 2009.

Eknath, Easwaran. *Passage Meditation: A Complete Spiritual Practice: Train Your Mind and Find a Life That Fulfills*. Nilgiri Press, 2016.

Eknath, Easwaran. *The Upanishads*. Nilgiri Press, 2007.

The Etymology of Passion - Owlcation. https://owlcation.com/humanities/The-Etymology-of-Passion.

Johnston, William. *The Cloud of Unknowing and The Book of Privy Counseling*. IMAGE Books, 1996.

Johnston, William. *The Mysticism of the Cloud of Unknowing*. Fordham University Press, 2005.

Kobell, Rona. "Glen Burnie Woman Named to President's Civic Service Council." *Baltimore Sun*, 30 Sept. 2021, https://www.baltimoresun.com/news/bs-xpm-2003-04-03-0304030323-story.html.

"Letter to the Bishops of the Catholic Church on Some Aspects of

Christian Meditation – Orationis Formas." *Vatican*, https://www.vatican.va/roman_curia/congregations/cfaith/documents/rc_con_cfaith_doc_19891015_meditazione-cristiana_en.html.

London, Daniel DeForest. *The Cloud of Unknowing, Distilled*. Apocryphile Press, 2021.

Newberg, Andrew. *How Enlightenment Changes Your Brain: The New Science of Transformation*. Avery Pub Group, 2017.

"Poverty of Spirit." *Ignatian Spirituality*, 27 Sept. 2021, https://www.ignatianspirituality.com/ignatian-prayer/the-spiritual-exercises/poverty-of-spirit/.

Rahula, Walpola Sri. "The Noble Eightfold Path: Meaning and Practice." *Tricycle*, 23 Nov. 2022, https://tricycle.org/magazine/noble-eightfold-path/.

Seneca, and Costa C D N (Translator). *On the Shortness of Life*. Penguin Books, 2005.

St. Augustine. *Confessions*. Oxford Univ. Press, 1998.

Thich Nhất Hạnh. *Silence: The Power of Quiet in a World Full of Noise*. HarperOne, 2016.

Trappists Brothers and Sisters. "Daily Reflection for December 18, 2022." *Cistercians of the Strict Observance (Trappists)*, 18 Dec. 2022, https://www.trappists.org/2022/12/18/daily-reflection-for-december-18-2022/.

"Tummo." *Tummo - Nangten Menlang International*, https://tulkulobsang.org/en/teachings/tummo#.

Wolters, Clifton. *The Cloud of Unknowing*. Penguin Books, 1977.

ABOUT THE AUTHOR

Mary Beth Bradford

Mary Beth Bradford moved to Lower, Slower Delaware to live a lower, slower life. She has a Ph.D. in mass communication and is a certified yoga and meditation instructor. Bradford is passionate about the common threads of various religious and spiritual traditions. She hopes to inspire others to answer the call of contemplation--or at least to live more simply and more kindly with others. She is deeply inspired by the mountains and the sea.

Printed in the USA
CPSIA information can be obtained
at www.ICGtesting.com
LVHW020223170624
783361LV00012B/821